BARBED
WIRE
FENCE

HAROLD LEWIS

ANGUS
& ROBERTSON

AN ANGUS & ROBERTSON BOOK

First published in Australia by
Angus & Robertson Publishers in 1973
Reprinted in 1973, 1974, 1975 (twice), 1977,
1979, 1981, 1983, 1985
Eden edition published in 1987
Reprinted in 1988 (twice)
This edition published by
Collins/Angus & Robertson Publishers Australia in 1990

Collins/Angus & Robertson Publishers Australia
Unit 4, Eden Park, 31 Waterloo Road, North Ryde
NSW 2113, Australia

William Collins Publishers Ltd
31 View Road, Glenfield, Auckland 10, New Zealand

Angus & Robertson (UK)
16 Golden Square, London W1R 4BN, United Kingdom

National Library of Australia
Cataloguing-in-Publication data:

Lewis, Harold, 1894–
  Crow on a barbed wire fence.

  ISBN 0 207 15801 0.

  1. Lewis, Harold, 1894– — Journeys — Australia.
  2. Country life — Australia. 3. Australia — Description
  and travel — 1901–1950. 4. Queensland — Description
  and travel — 1901–1950. 5. Australia — Social life
  and customs — 1901–1914. I. Title.

307.72

Cover illustration: North Queensland Stockman *by Ray Crooke.*
Printed by The Book Printer, Victoria

18 17 16 15 14
95 94 93 92 91 90

A few words before we begin

THE FIRST THING that struck me about *Crow On A Barbed Wire Fence* was its title. With a name like that, it couldn't be anything but Australian! In detailing his adventures as a young man in Outback Australia just before the First World War, Harold Lewis has captured the feeling of a time when swaggies, quartpots and "Jimmy Woodsers" were part of our language and heritage. With remarkable descriptive power he brings his colleagues, and the fabulous characters who cross their adventurous paths, to life.

He takes us on a rollicking adventure from Narrabri and Moree, in the northwest of New South Wales, up to Brisbane, where he dabbles in the art of punting at The Creek (for the uninitiated, that's Brisbane's famed Albion Park racecourse); then out to the vast southwest of Queensland, through Roma, Charleville and Cunnamulla; from there, north to the sugar country around Bundaberg, "The Proserpine" and Mackay; back south briefly to Rockhampton; then out to the central west, to the gem fields of Emerald and Anakie; and further out still to the start of the sheep country and to places with names like Bogantungan, Barcaldine and Longreach.

Crow On A Barbed Wire Fence is a rousing reminiscence of an era—and of a way of life—which is now, sadly, a bygone one. Regardless of whether you're a Bananabender, a Cornstalk, a Croweater, a Sandgroper, a Taswegian or a Whatever-they-call-people-who-live-south-of-the-Murray, you're going to enjoy this book. And whatever you do, don't lend it to a friend. Chances are you won't get it back . . . and you'll be stuck there like a crow on a barbed wire fence!

GARRY ORD
Brisbane

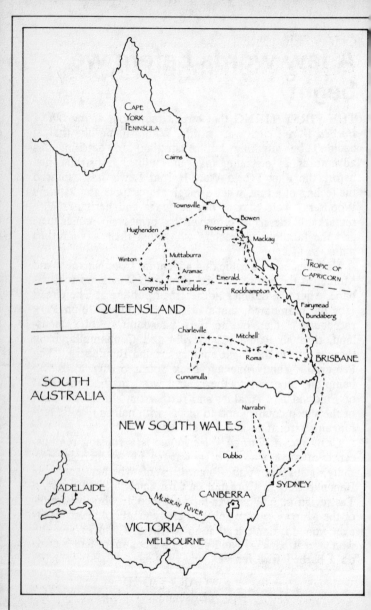

Bluey's Travels

CHAPTER ONE
Strike me bloody hooray!

IT WAS the flock of galahs, with their vividly pink under-wings, rising from the scrub near the railway halt as we climbed down from the train, that inspired the first joyous awareness that I was here at last, in the country of my many dreams, the country of the phoney brochures. Now I saw it, smelt it, felt its heat, tasted the dry air.

From Sydney in an express train travelling at twenty miles an hour, I had sweated through a day and a night in the long coach. I had squirmed under the curious, con-temptuous, yet perhaps sympathetic eyes of Australian outbackers going back, and had listened to the rasping criticisms of my companion, the paunchy mill hand from Huddersfield.

The scene beyond the large wide windows had varied little once the towns were left behind—vast, grey-green plains, dotted with bush growth and with great gum trees, some broad and powerful as an English oak, others tall and stately, their smooth peeling bark glistening blue-grey-white. There were no hedgerows, no cottages, no copses, no end to any view; otherwise it could have been one of England's flatter counties; except that the colour motif was blue—a flat, water-colour blue.

The halt was disappointing. I had travelled 12,000 miles to Sydney, and another 400 odd miles north-west, to find my destination nothing more than a shed and a post with a string mail sack. There were no porters, no railway officials at all. The place had no name board. The guard walked along the track to our coach, shouted out "Narrabri!" and we climbed down the steps, I with my large leather case, the Yorkshireman with a gladstone bag, a large parcel and a wooden box.

Before alighting, I put on my hat, the broadbrimmed, wideawake scouts type specially bought for me by my

Uncle George, and my companion crammed his hard bowler hat firmly on his head, hitched his pants and rattled the silver medals dangling from his heavy watch chain. And we each said in turn, to the dozen or so men in the coach, "Well, thanks, gentlemen. Good morning", or something like that. The only reply reached my ears when, I like to think, we were considered out of earshot. It was simply: "Gawd strike me dead."

It was an expression I was to hear several times a day from then onward, varied according to how the pleader desired to be struck. It might be pink, or up a gum tree, or it might be hooray.

I had been reared in a strict Methodist home, with chapel three times on Sundays, Band of Hope on Mondays, Christian Endeavour on Wednesdays and choir practice on Fridays, and as I was barely sixteen some time passed before I managed to equate myself with bush language. Later on, I was able, without too much remorse, to say: "Well, strike me hooray". It was a satisfying, meaningless expression and I hoped I would not be eternally damned for using it. The man in the train, I felt at the time, was taking a terrible chance of being heard.

The galahs were beautiful, a brilliant conception of nature in sharp green and grey, with a mulberry pink underneath as they rose. There were probably a hundred or more, slightly larger than starlings, and as we stood there by the shed which was the halt, with our train pulling slowly away towards Moree, the galahs rose again and wheeled, showing off.

"Not a bloody soul in sight," said the man from Huddersfield. "It shows you. No organisation. Ah've been brung all the way from Huddersfield to this dummed 'ole to work for one pound a week, and no one to greet me. I'll not stand for it. That I'll not."

"Perhaps they never had the message, Mr Bloom," I ventured. "Shall we walk?"

"Walk?" he shouted. "Walk? Where'd you walk to in this desert? It could be fifty mile away."

A few minutes later two men drove up the track in a

buggy and found us. One, a young man who had shaved, looked keenly at us. "You the two from the Sydney Labour Office?"

His companion, of indeterminate age, unshaven, looked us over with widening eyes. What he said was: "Gawd strike me bloody hooray." This, perhaps, was the ultimate in bush comment.

We climbed into the back of the buggy, which had no seats, and clung to the sides as the unshaven one cracked a short-handled whip and gave a cry like a half-strangled screech owl. The buggy jerked into movement and we sped down the uneven track, through blue grass and scrub, rocking from side to side and leaving in our wake a curtain of red dust. Mr Bloom soon realised the impossibility of keeping his bowler hat on his head, and I removed my splendid scout's wideawake, the hot wind driving through my ginger hair. We drove by shakes and bumps for thirty miles, with a single interlude: we came to a gate in a wire fence, the first and only fence in the journey.

"Open the gate, one of you," said the alert-eyed young man.

I climbed down, lifted the wire loop off the top of the gate and let it swing open. The buggy drove through and I climbed in.

This drew a very long sentence consisting entirely of oaths, imprecations and pleas to the Almighty from the unshaven driver. His companion, whom I now saw clearly to be the boss, said quietly: "The gate, Bluey. Always shut gates."

"Yes, sir," I said.

From the remarks the driver addressed to the horses, I knew that I had made another mistake. There were no sirs in these parts.

We spent the night at the wooden bungalow of a boundary rider, and it was here that we joined the rest of the team, ten Australian bush hands. None was under forty, so far as I could tell. All were burnt dark brown, muscular, lean of face. To us, Mr Bloom and me, they had nothing to say at first. In their faces was the same expression as in

3

those of the men we had journeyed with in the train, the same thought as that so violently expressed by our driver.

Our appearance staggered them and it was obviously their opinion that we were of no use in Australia, ought never to have come, and ought to go home forthwith. To me, this meant that there was something I had to make clear at the earliest opportunity, but for the moment I said nothing. I was a boy; easily abashed. This new world offered no welcome, no greeting, to us.

At six, close to sundown, we had supper. I took my tin plate and my tin pannikin to the cook, and returned to a corner of the verandah with a pile of chops, some bread, a bottle of tomato sauce and a pint of strong hot tea without milk or sugar. I was also told to pick a tin of IXL jam, and dwelt with a boy's delight on the labels—peach, apricot, melon and ginger, quince, pineapple.

The tea was difficult to take, tasting of tin, but bitterly refreshing in this hot country, and I was to learn that in the bush, milk was never available, potatoes and an onion for the cook came out occasionally, that sugar with tea was a mistake, though available, and that the staple diet was bread and meat.

A sheep was killed for the team each day—usually chops for breakfast, cold boiled shoulders for dinner, hot roast legs for tea. The cook made yeast bread in an iron pan covered with hot wood ash. It was suicide to complain about the cooking. On the other hand, if the tomato sauce ran out, the men would demand their "time" and cut out of the job.

After supper, I waited for Mr Bloom to make the first move. He hitched his pants, rattled his football medals and walked over to the fire. The team sat around. I noticed every man sat on one heel, so I sat on one heel and found it painful after about three minutes. Nevertheless, this was something I would have to master, for it was the way men sat in this country.

The ganger, the cleanshaven young man who had met us, had some papers in his hand. He read them by the glow of the fire and said: "This," thumbing at Mr Bloom, "is Joe.

And this is—what's this one?—We'll call you Bluey. That's a good Australian name for ginger tops."

"Thank you, sir," I said, filled with pride.

He started to correct me, changed his mind and walked away.

The man from Huddersfield filled his pipe with strong shag, and when he had done pressing it down one of the team took a burning piece of wood from the fire and handed it to him. It was the first gesture of acknowledgment.

"This burr cutting," said Mr Bloom. "What's a burr? Back home we call a thistle a burr."

"That's right," said the Australian. "You'll see it tomorrow, soon as we pitch camp.'

"Quickest I ever saw," an Australian was saying in the firelight glow, "was on a cocky selection north of Moree. Three of us was burning off timber which had bin ringbarked, and some of it was already down and rotting. Man name of Chapman, from Melb'n. He was sett'n on an old log cutting a chew when a redbacked spider walked off his sleeve onto his hand. He shook it off, but it bit him first. We tried to dig out the poison, but he was dead in less than half an hour."

"Always liable to find them red-backs in old wood," said the man sitting on a heel next to me. He turned to me. "You seen a red-back spider, chum?"

"No," I said, startled to be spoken to. 'How big is it?"

"No size at all. Maybe half an inch long. He's black, like lamp black, with a red line down the middle of his back. You just out from the Old Country, chum?"

"Yes."

"Like 'Stralia?"

"Very much," I said and was glad I said it, for there was a touch of challenge in his question. "It looks wonderful."

He looked at my pale, freckled face and white hands. "Well, you watch yourself, chum. It can be bloody hot tomorrow." After which he ignored me.

I lay that night, like the others, on the verandah floor. Sleep was not possible—I had never slept on a wooden floor with nothing else under me except my blanket. I wondered whether one undressed in these circumstances, and thought not. So I lay fully dressed except for my shoes. My bones ached; I was a tall, frail, skinny youth, having shot up like a plant struggling for light.

I lay on the boards with my thoughts. What was ahead held no fears for me. Strange, this, for I was a timid boy, afraid of spiders, afraid of the dark, afraid of bullies, afraid of the unseen and the unknown. Yet I had craved this adventure with a desperate enthusiasm which overcame the fears and objections of my parents, and when I left the security of my home I had no uneasiness.

Now I thought of people I knew. I must write home as soon as possible. The letter would take six or eight weeks. I wondered about the three friends I had made on the voyage, three young men all older than myself, who accepted me. They had gone on to Queensland and had vowed they would stick together. I must write to them.

There was Ted, an unemployed electrician from a London tram depot. Ted had left England because he knew he could never get another job, though he had not said why this was. Ted was fully ten years older than myself, a small, dark, short-sighted, wiry chap, with a bitter outlook on life. Ted had treated me as a noodle and a nuisance, and any remarks he made to me or about me in my hearing were shot with heavy sarcasm. Yet I felt he was a man I could trust, and as he seemed as ill-equipped as I was for this adventure I thought a good deal about him that night. A tram electrician's mate in the Australian bush!

The others would be a success anywhere. Hugh was nineteen, a laughing, curly-headed giant son of a Bedfordshire farmer, with self-assurance, muscles, good looks. Around this camp fire he would have known everyone within a few minutes. The third in the group was in his early twenties and already a man whose personality was deeply etched. His sharply set, light blue eyes were calculating, often suspicious. He rarely laughed, though at times he made wry jokes. He seemed to have come from a good family, much above my own class, and said his name was Jack Hart. I was in awe of Hart, though I could have given

6

no reason.

These were my shipboard friends in a time when I had sorely needed friends. We four, and Mr Bloom, were mere numbers in a vast agglomeration of humanity being shipped week by week from the British Isles to Australia—men, women, families; young, middle-aged and old. Most went because they were sick of unemployment and near-starvation. Some, for adventure, others expecting to make a fortune quickly, and a few for reasons never disclosed as, for instance, Hart.

Most were from what were called the lower and lower-middle classes, and what they paid for their journey depended on their trade. A carpenter could go for ten pounds, a farm worker for one pound, and if he hadn't a pound they shipped him free. Twelve to a cabin, many of them, six and eight to a cabin for those who paid or paid a little, they left Tilbury and Liverpool and Southampton in thousands every week. This was 1910, before the Dole.

Mr Bloom I first met when, at Tilbury, I found my way through the below-deck smell of hot engine oil to the cabin for six to which I was allotted. I sat on my bunk, with my leather case beside me, savouring the most exciting moment of my life. Why I should want to leave my family I could never explain even to myself, but the fact that it was at last accomplished gave me a sensation of enormous triumph.

Mr Bloom came in, said "Hullo" to me, put a straw-matted grip on the opposite lower bunk, and staggered out. He was already drunk. The grip fell open, and I was horrified to see that it was full of bottles of beer. Shades of Monday night Band of Hope! Until that moment when I looked at the labels, I had never seen a bottle of beer at close quarters.

CHAPTER TWO
Among the bushwhackers

BEFORE DAWN the cook was stirring the fire and throwing on fresh logs, and I was glad to get up, stiff and chilled. The sky was the colour of blue-black ink, the stars larger and brighter than I had ever seen. Men around me were moving, pulling on trousers—they had undressed, I noted —and took their towels to the galvanised water tank at one corner of the bungalow.

I also washed, and came back to my leather bag. In that bag was my most prized possession, a pair of light brown leather leggings. These were another gift from my Uncle George, and I had put them on many times when alone. This seemed the right moment for them to appear in public, although it was a Sunday morning. Uncle George, a poker-faced Cockney comic at the popular smoking concerts around Islington, Holborn and Euston, had a boot-and-shoe shop opposite King's Cross Station in London and was therefore regarded in my family as a wealthy man. He fitted me out—proud, I think, to have a nephew mad enough to leave home so young on such an adventure—with every leather article I might need: my boots and shoes, my leather bag, my secret money belt, my case of hair brushes and these priceless, beautiful, romantic leggings. The wideawake hat was also his idea.

With some trepidation I put on the leggings and my wideawake hat, and with the rest of the team answered the cook's banging on a tin plate. The sun was sending the first long, low streaks of golden light across the horizon. I was last in the queue, behind the man from Huddersfield. He had shed his coat but not his waistcoat, nor his chain and medals, nor his highcrowned hard hat.

The Australians wore no coats. Their hats were small-brimmed soft felts, very old and stained, and punched in at the crown. They all wore singlets of grey flannel without sleeves, and dungaree trousers. No one spoke to us. The cook loaded our tin plates with solid hunks of minced mutton, the size of tennis balls, and we filled our pannikins from the tea pail.

The ganger came over. He had already shaved. "You men ride a horse?"

Mr Bloom shook his head morosely. He was not happy. I decided I would do a little better, and said: "Not yet, but I can try. I have to learn, haven't I?"

The ganger hesitated.

"Give the kid a horse, Mr Carter," said the cook.

"Not yet, Snowy," said the ganger coldly. "He might kill himself. The company wants something for its money. You two ride on the rations wagon. And Bluey, it'll be hot," and his glance roved significantly over my attire.

So I took off my coat, rolled up my sleeves and exposed my thin white arms to the warming sun. With mixed relief and reluctance I also put away my beautiful leggings, and never wore them again. Leggings were not worn in the bush, but this I would never be able to tell my Uncle George.

We travelled until four in the afternoon, and pitched our camp near a large, man-made dam, about fifty yards square, dug out and lined with clay. It was half-full of water, covered with green scum and littered with the bleached skeletons of animals which had stuck in the clay mud and died in the sun, watched by the crows awaiting the final quiver.

The speed with which the camp was made was a miracle in my eyes. With short axes, the Australians cut saplings, trimmed them to size, put up a row of tiny tents, made a dining table, benches, a roof of foliage, and a shelter from the burning sun for the cook. The cook had his galley up and his great pots swinging over a fire of logs, and before dark all that was left to do was the making of beds, by laying saplings and covering them with soft brush.

My own part was one of fetching and carrying, but every man made his own bed. They all paired off until two tents were left. Into one of these went Mr Bloom, with his parcel, his box and his gladstone bag, and into the other went a

9

swarthy Australian. With one of these I must pair. It was a chance to leave Mr Bloom.

"Would you mind if I shared your tent?" I asked the Australian.

He glared at me aggressively. "Would I mind! Bloody hell," he said, and turned away.

"Thank you," I said meekly and dumped my bag on the grass. I got myself an axe, hewed out some saplings, feeling like a woman must feel when she first holds a cricket bat, and made my bed. I felt I was learning.

I stayed on that job six full months, during which time I suffered physical agonies, a chronic longing for the things I had left behind, and the knowledge that I was held by the Australians in a contempt which was savagely hurtful at times, yet which I felt was on the surface only.

Each morning, after a dawn breakfast, we went out with heavy hoes, spread in a line ten or twenty yards apart, and cut the offending burr bush. The hoe tired me, and the sun burnt my unprotected arms so badly that they swelled to double size and had to be bandaged. Foolishly, I had cut the sleeves off my shirt to be as much like the Australians as possible. My hands were blistered.

The great ugly frill lizards frightened me until an Australian taunted me by putting one on my shoulder. I met snakes. I had dreamt of snakes. "There's only one snake in these parts likely to hurt you," said the ganger, "and he's called the death adder. He strikes so quick you'll never see him, so don't worry."

He gave me my chance to ride, after a few weeks. We had thirty miles to go, through the night. The first horse given me threw me and fractured a bone in a wrist. I said nothing, because I was afraid of being sacked. Then the ganger put me on a quiet old lady, and I bumped along on a wet saddle through the rain until I was so sore I was in tears. I was thankful for the dark.

I missed most the things of boyhood—sweets above all. The cook made cakes one Sunday, having been issued with a few currants, but I was the only customer. Sweet things, fruit, I craved. I tried to make a sweet liquor with some pennyroyal I found growing, but it was undrinkable. There was no solace for me in smoking or drinking, because I was not yet a man, though attempting to masquerade as one, taking the earnings of a man, and trying to do the work expected of a man. My father, a sworn teetotaller and non-smoker, had tried to be wise by presenting me, before I started my journey, with a small meerschaum pipe ("not so bad as cigarettes," he said).

It was a pretty pipe, carved, and, with its clay bowl still in pristine white and its outside coat of shining yellow, it demanded to be smoked and coloured. I still had with me what was left of the single ounce of "Country Life" tobacco I had bought on the ship, and one night when the chronic, bone-piercing tiredness and burning of the day's labour had subsided, I joined the group around the fire, as permitted by the cook when meals were finished, sat on one heel and filled my pipe.

The pipe excited attention. I was flattered as it was passed from hand to hand and admired. My own tent partner, known as Africa because he talked incessantly of the time when he worked in the diamond fields, was loud in his praises. He handed me a kindled stick and asked to see my tobacco. That, too, aroused interest. It was tested for making cigarettes and was soon finished.

The next night Africa handed me his cake of Yankee Doodle and his knife. I had watched the Australians and had some idea how to cut thin slivers from the solid cake of tobacco, tease it and stuff it into the bowl; but I found it impossible to keep alight, and the steady sucking in of the powerful fumes made me sick. I had some way to go before I could cope with Yankee Doodle. The pipe did me a great service, however, for it had the effect of making Africa somewhat conversational.

Mr Bloom, though fiercely retaining his Yorkshire identity and earning some hectic opprobrium by his pride of his town, his trade, his country and his countrymen, had nevertheless become accepted. He could swing his hoe, for one thing. He was also of mature age and opinion, and he would cross swords with the cook himself. I was the failure.

I could not do my stint. Physical prowess was almost everything here. Nor could I stand up for myself in any way. No one asked my opinion, and no one answered me if I ventured one.

But the meerschaum pipe cracked the ice. Africa examined it several times, pointed out that it would improve both in colour and in smoking pleasure the more it was used, and asked if he might try one pipe. To me, this was joy.

One Sunday, after the usual washing of pants and shirts, someone said: "Who's going for papers? The railroad is only five miles west and a train goes through this afternoon."

I was one of three volunteers. We walked through the trackless bush to the railroad and sat and waited for the train. Then we spread out and yelled. A shower of newspapers, copies of the Sydney *Bulletin* and farm journals were hurled at us, and these we bore back to camp in triumph. The advertisements fascinated me, for I was earning real money for the first time in my life. It was accumulating, and I could speculate on the glorious feeling of sending for a self measurement form for a made-to-measure suit for fifty shillings.

On the following Sunday, Africa made a staggering suggestion. A little further along the line, maybe eight miles from camp, he said, was a halt, and by the halt was a pub. He would take me there, if I liked. I leapt at the chance, for I hoped there might also be a store, where I might buy oranges, chocolates or biscuits.

But there was just a pub, and not a soul in sight as we walked into the cool bar, except the publican. We stood up to the bar. Africa looked at me. I had given the matter a great deal of thought during the walk and knew exactly what I was going to order.

"Port and lemon, please," I said. I had tasted this once and it seemed not unpleasant.

Africa drew a deep breath, and grunted: "Pint."

I put my sixpence on the counter, and he put down a shilling and invited the publican to drink. Everything was sixpence. One port and lemon was enough for me, though I liked its sweetness. Africa had half-a-dozen pints in quick succession and we started back towards camp. I sensed he was angry, grimly angry, but I dared not ask why.

After two or three miles in silence, walking at great pace, he suddenly stopped and said: "Bluey, I nearly killed you."

"Yes," I said, "I knew you were angry, Africa, but I don't know why."

"You don't know why?"

"No."

"You ever had a drink before?"

"No," I said, "I never have. What did I do wrong?"

He walked in silence for another half mile, and then said: "Stone the crows. God stone the bloody crows."

I said nothing. He spoke no more until we went to bed that night, and then, before he put out the carbide lamp, he sat up as if with a great effort, and said: "Bluey, never drink another Jimmy Woodser as long as you live."

"You mean that port and lemon, Africa?"

"I mean drinkin' by yourself. No man drinks by himself."

"Oh," I said. "Thanks, Africa. Thanks very much."

That incident did something to humanise Africa. "A man can be too long in the bush," he said one evening later. "A man's mind gets into a groove. All a man gets to thinkin' about is booze and tarts."

He then told me about his life in South Africa, laced with the crudest of stories about his women. He was going back, he said, back to South Africa, away out of the Australian bush for ever. That was a remark I heard from many a man in the next few years. They were always just going down to the coast at long last, and out of the bush for ever. I wondered sometimes whether it would be my fate to be held in the outback by the same intangible thrall; a weakness of the will betraying the wishes of the mind.

This part of the bush, at any rate, I was leaving, for as the job was finishing I had wonderful news, a letter from Jack Hart, one of my three shipboard friends. He was in Brisbane, with a fine job, and he thought I could get myself a job in the city quite easily and earn enough to keep myself.

I was so happy I worked like an Australian that last week, slashing away with my great hoe, singing as I went. I carried the great four-gallon wire-handled kerosene water cans for the cook and ventured to ask him to show me how to make bread without yeast.

"It's taken a long time, Bluey," said the ganger, "but you're almost earning your tucker at last."

I survived those first months simply because there was no escape, no turning back, no going home, no one even to take me to the rail halt. For all I knew, I could have starved, or been bushed without water, if I had given in. I had been burnt a bright red, my skin had hardened like cracked parchment and my face was mottled with red and freckles. I had lived in strong air, eaten large quantities of meat and bread. I had tortured my soft little muscles until they were numb, and I was desperate with fatigue and the heat. And I had had to face the fact that I was committing a fraud by taking the job, and all the camp knew it and resented it.

There was still that one matter I had determined to clear up, and this I did on the last night before we cut out. My chance came when a man said to Mr Bloom: "Where are you going next, Yorksheer?"

"Ah'm goin' 'ome, out of this dum 'ole as fast as I can, mate," he said. "Ah'll be better off out o' work in Huddersfield."

"What the hell did you come here for?" was the angry retort.

This was almost a nightly scene. "We Australians have to pay taxes to bring useless bastards over here like you and Bluey—."

"Not me," I said, jumping up and coming right into the middle of the group. This was something I had always wanted to say. "Not me. My father paid my fare, every penny of it. Twenty-seven pounds."

"Well," was the gently sneering retort. "Let's hope he pays your fare back to the Old Country."

"He would," I shouted shrilly. "But I'm not going back!" I stood my full six feet and my full eight stone quivered.

14

"I'm staying in bloody Australia."

Just for a few seconds the air around the camp fire was alive with "By cripes", "Hoorah, Bluey" and "Strike me dead". Then someone said "Four-hander of crib?" and the party broke up. But just for those few seconds I had tasted triumph, though triumph over what I didn't quite know.

I asked the cook what it was like in Queensland.

"You goin' to Queensland, Bluey?"

"Well, I have friends there. Is it good in Queensland, Snowy? Better than here in New South?"

The white-haired cook turned his lined face to me as he kneaded his dough, and squinted at me from under his upper eyelids, as Australians do after a life under the southern sun.

"Depends what you want, Bluey."

I thought that over. "Yes, I suppose so."

"Well," he said, unexpectedly leading the conversation, "what in hell do you want? What d'ya come out here for?"

I sat on my heel and pondered. Then I said: "Snowy, I never asked myself that question, but I believe the answer is that I didn't want to stay in London any more. I wanted the open air. Oh, yes, and I wanted the warmth. I've been cold all my life, I think, until I came out here. Then, again, I wanted to make a lot of money, but I wanted to make it out here, and to make a home here for my parents."

He dealt the dough a mighty punch at that. "Well, stone me pink," he said. "Stone me bloody pink. You goin' to make a fortune cuttin' burrs at a pound a week?"

"I've got nearly twenty pounds saved, Snowy," I said. "That's more money than I ever thought I'd have all at the same time, I can tell you, cobber. I'm going on working and saving until I can buy a farm, and then my old man and my mother will come out and live on the farm but not have to do any work. That is, unless they want to pick a few peaches and pears, and maybe gather some eggs for breakfast. I reckon I'll have a mixed farm, bit of everything, you know, and buy more and more land, and build it all up. Like other people have."

"Like hell," said the cook. "You a farmer?"

"No," I said, "but I've read a lot about it."

He almost smiled at that. "Bluey," he said, 'if you was a good farmer, and if you had a bunch of money, say ten thousand pounds, or even five thousand, you cud go down to Victoria and start you a mixed farm and it cud all be bosker. But you ain't a farmer and you got twenty pounds."

"Well," I said, "I had rather thought it was a bit like that. But people do come here and make good money, don't they?"

"If you was an engine driver," he said, "or a fully trained carpenter, or even a good cook who didn't get on the booze, you could make a good living in any part of any state in 'Stralia. But the country's overrun with coves like you, unskilled blokes from the Old Country expectin' to make a fortune. Listen, Bluey," he said earnestly, "if you cud make a fortune, so cud I."

"Yes, I see that. You think I ought to go home, don't you?"

"Me?" He knocked the dough about for quite a while. Then, without looking at me he said, "I think you should go to Queensland."

"You do?"

"Newer state, more things opening up, bigger demand for labour. Never know what you'll find in Queensland. Might even find your fortune there. Try it all, Bluey. Try the sugar country above all. There's money in the sugar country. There certainly is money up there in the Proserpine. Stone me, I might go up there myself when I cut out from here."

To the ganger, the permanent hand who shaved every morning, I diffidently offered my leggings. He was plainly shocked, but accepted in a warm, friendly way. Two other signs of the newchum I resolved to discard. One was that hat, and this I flung out of the railway coach as we left the siding.

It was my second performance of this act, for I had left my home in London in my Sunday suit and wearing my little bowler hat, and as the train pulled out of Fenchurch Street Station I sent the bowler skimming away across the rails as a gesture of a newborn recklessness. The other part of my equipment which would have to go was the costly leather bag. Alas! Uncle George. In the bush one carried a swag, a blanket rolled around all one's clothes and other possessions. A swag, a billycan and a waterbag. No leather cases.

In the train, going down to Sydney, I missed my meer-schaum pipe. Its new owner was an easy guess. Well, he was welcome to it, if only for a parting handshake, offered with misgiving as he said "I wish you luck, cobber, fair dinkum I do," before he shuffled up the track to Moree. Africa wasn't going to the coast yet, he said. Africa was making for the nearest pub, with his cheque.

SYDNEY hadn't changed much, but I had. I knew all about Gilberts. Gilberts had little restaurants dotted around. There were sixpenny Gilberts, ninepenny Gilberts and shilling Gilberts. In Gilberts you could have a three-course breakfast, dinner or "tea" for the price. When I found my first Gilberts at seven o'clock in the morning of my arrival from England, with less than thirty shillings in the world, I elected for the sixpenny three-course breakfast. They said in the bush that the more you paid the more flies you got.

My first meal in Sydney, three courses for sixpence, was a plate of porridge, two huge sausages, unlimited bread, butter and jam, and tea. Coming back, rich, I went right out for the shilling luxury meal. They served me soup, a large steak with two fried eggs on top, all the trimmings, a sweet, and tea which came with the soup. After six months of mutton this was one of the truly memorable meals of my life.

Passing a pub, a shabby Australian lurched up to me and said: "Givus a traybit." He didn't ask, and he wasn't rude. He requested, in the manner of one completely within his rights. I gave him the threepence and he turned into the pub without thanking me. I knew now that a man could ask a stranger for threepence and be given it without favours shown. For threepence he could get a pint of beer and a free meal—the famous Sydney counter lunch.

All drinks in Sydney were threepence. All drinks in the

bush were sixpence in a town with a railway running through it. All drinks "off the line", or "in the Never-Never" were a shilling. Threepence was a traybit, sixpence was a zack and a shilling was a dinar. I was pleased to have been "requested" for a traybit. It made me feel part of the Australian scene.

CHAPTER THREE
Low life in Brisbane

HART MET ME on the wharf at Brisbane as I stepped off the ship from Sydney. It was noon on a Saturday. He was agitated and in a great hurry.

"You had lunch?"

"Not yet."

"Oh, hell. Well, I'll show you where you eat while I put your bag in the station cloakroom. You've got money, haven't you?"

"Nearly twenty pounds, Jack. Do you think I should bank it?"

"Bank it?" He paused. "You give me that money. We're going to double it and treble it this afternoon. You'll see."

I soon saw. We were going to the races, going to The Creek. He was going to put my money on the horses, and this was something which I had heard vaguely referred to in church services as one of the major evils of mankind.

"You mean we're going to gamble, Jack? Back horses? But that's a frightful thing to do, isn't it?"

"It is," he said, "if you lose. I happen to know some horses which are going to win. Don't worry."

I saw him give two of my pounds to a bookmaker before the first race, scanned the programme frantically to try to identify our horse, and was shattered when it came in with a bunch of others, well behind the winner.

Hart soothed me, but not too gently. I had the impression he was being considerate about my boyish ignorance but that the stony realness of his nature was not far beneath. We had a succession of losers. Each time Hart was briefly reassuring that the next one would come up, and only by frantic gymnastics was I able to watch my money being handed over and keep a rough tally of it as it disappeared. The racing might have excited me, and the gambling might have thrilled me, but for the tragedy, belting into my mind with shattering emphasis, race after race, that all my money, the first I had ever earned, the foundation of my fortune-to-be, was slipping away.

I wondered what my Dad would have said, my little Dad, the shepherd boy from the hills in South Wales, who taught himself to read and write, came to London, and slaved for his family. My Dad, whose only extravagance was giving more than he could afford to any charity that approached him. To my Dad it was a sin even to discuss horse racing.

I marched with others from our Methodist church many a Sunday evening, and stood in the circle around him while he preached on the evils of racing, billiard saloons, whist drives and dance halls. We prayed for their total extinction, but my father had a special prayer for the souls of the billiard players. Perhaps this was because we had a little billiard table ourselves.

I had written home about my savings. Writing home hadn't been easy, for there was a good deal I couldn't tell without shocking my parents, and a good deal I must leave out lest they imagine the life was killing or depraving me. So I wrote about my successes. I had ridden a horse—now that was something for a boy from a London dormitory of terraced houses behind iron railings and privet.

I had tried to break it gently that I hadn't managed to get a job on a farm, and that the farm idea was not glowing quite so brightly as one came closer to it. But at the same time I did have all this money, and if I could go on getting jobs and stacking the money away it wouldn't be long before we'd have that farm.

Such thoughts chased each other within my mind as I followed my friend Hart around the ring of bookmakers and then took up a place whence I could see the blur of horses racing by, and read the tell-tale figures on the results board.

When the last race came Hart had three pounds of my money left, and he put it on a horse which started at twelve to one. It was a mare called Destruction, and I saw it lead the field with a tremendous spurt. I saw it being steadily overhauled by two others, a furlong from home. I saw the collision as these two fought to overtake and I saw the whole of the rest of the field thrown out of stride and Destruction win by twenty lengths.

My throat was dry and I realised I was hoarse with shouting. Hart watched the race coolly. He bought me some beer, which I was unable to finish, and when we were in our lodgings he said: "I kept telling you we would come out winning. You never need worry when you're with me. It just had to work out for us."

"But the horse might have lost, Jack, but for that collision."

"Yes, it might. But then two others we backed ought to have won with ordinary luck. Just remember this: to win at racing you have to know horses and have a sound system of betting. Then you must win."

"And do you know horses, Jack?"

"My uncle owns a stud," he said.

"What's a stud?"

"A stud is a horse farm, where they breed racehorses like those we saw today."

I was impressed. "Then you could go on winning, and putting more and more on, and make a fortune?"

He looked at me sharply. "That's the general idea," he said.

He showed me the town that Saturday night, and I believe he was as careful as he could be to shield me from experiences I might regret. What happened was like his racing results: sooner or later it had to work out.

Just before midnight, we were in the long bar of O'Byrne's. I was happy, sleepy, still excited, and had had a very small amount of liquor—enough, perhaps, to get me into trouble. There were forty or fifty men in the smoke-laden bar, mostly from the racing at The Creek, mostly half-drunk, drunk, or dead drunk.

All around me were Australians talking Australian. Nearly everything was a fair cow, occasionally something was a bonzer. People mentioned in their absence were bastards, whether friend or foe. The barmen were rushing about, glasses were crashing off the bar counter, arguments were rising and falling, and once a man was lifted bodily and flung through the swing doors. He came staggering back, his face bleeding, full of fight though he looked no more than six stone, and was led quietly away by his friends. The life of the long bar was resumed.

"We'll have one and go home," said Jack.

His remark was overheard by an enormous man in a singlet, whose great tattooed forearms were massive with flexing muscles. He clamped one huge hand like a vice on Hart's shoulder and turned him round like a doll.

"You'll buy me a drink, too, newy. Hey! Feller with a white face is buyin' drinks!'

Only a dozen or so heard him in the din, and few took any notice.

"Let's all have drinks with the boy with the white face!"

He banged his other great fist on the bar.

That gave Hart room for movement. He twisted out of the big man's grip and in the same action seized a tankard from the counter and crashed it into the big man's temple. It all took no more than a second. I had never seen a man fall just like that. He fell against the bar, hit his head hard on the brass foot rail, and shook the floor.

"Let's get out," said Jack and pushed me by the elbow. But it wasn't so simple. The big man had friends. We had none. I can remember someone coming towards me, and I know that I squared up in the approved Jem Mace fashion. Then I was jolted into the dark of unconsciousness, and for me the fight was over.

I awoke on a pleasant Sunday morning. I was in a soft bed, stripped to my skin. The blind was still drawn and there was a closeness in the room and a smell of a woman's things. My head ached violently and I felt a little sick. My left eye was in pain, and I felt a large bruise on the cheekbone.

But I wasn't unhappy. I lay there and wondered where I was, how I got there, where Jack was, and why I was in a very nice double bed.

The door opened slightly, then wider, and a girl came in.

She smiled at me, and I thought she was quite easily the most beautiful girl, and the nicest, I had ever seen anywhere. Not my age group—maybe twenty-five or even thirty. Charming in a female way, yet not motherly. I couldn't analyse it.

I started to say something.

"Like some breakfast? Ham and eggs?"

She vanished. Amid the mystery of it all I was acutely aware that this was the first time I had heard an Australian woman speak with an Australian accent. Curious thing to remember.

It was a good breakfast. I washed and dressed, and she put some cream on the purple bruise on my cheekbone.

"I seen them throw you out of O'Byrne's," she said, "so I brung you home."

"How?"

"In a cab. Cabby feller I know. Comes here. No money in yer pockets, Bluey."

Funny, the way everyone called me Bluey.

"No, Hart's got it all. How'd you know my name's Bluey?"

"Easy guess."

"And who . . . did you put me to bed?"

She laughed. "I've put a lot of 'em to bed, Bluey," she said. Then she added quickly, "Here's a couple of shills to get you home. Now run off."

"But I owe you something, miss," I said. "You've been very good to me."

She stared at me and I fancied she swore quietly.

"What's your name?" I asked.

"Sheila," she said. "Just Sheila." She opened the door and pushed me out. "S'long, Bluey. Good luck on yer."

I found myself standing outside a pretty little bungalow called "Taplow". Taplow, a place on the Thames near Burnham Beeches, where I went once when very small.

I could see the Brisbane River, and guessed I was on the wrong side of the bridge, so I crossed the bridge, came into Brisbane, past O'Byrne's, already open again on this beautiful Sunday morning, and so through the city and up the Hill upon which was the great cluster of wood and iron houses where most of Brisbane lived.

I found my lodgings, and I found Hart.

"I lost you in the scramble last night," he said.

I told him a lady named Sheila had kindly taken me to her home.

He looked at me with an odd expression. "Was she young?"

"Yes, I think so."

"Did you pay her anything?"

"She didn't ask me. Anyway I hadn't any money. She gave me two bob to get home. Jolly decent, don't you think?"

"Jolly decent," he said. "She'll be at least thirty shillings out of pocket. I'll see she gets it back. By the way, keep out of O'Byrne's for a bit. Three men are in gaol. It developed into a general scrap, and before I could fight my way through the doors to find you, you'd been picked up."

"Good heavens!" I said, dismayed. "We might have been in gaol too!"

"That," said Hart, "is something you will not have to worry about. I work in the office of the Commissioner of Police."

BRISBANE was a city growing too fast to grow properly. From the quayside inwards were well-designed, clean lined commercial buildings such as one might find just built around Leadenhall Street in London, but on straight, broader streets. A couple of blocks, and one was in the main thoroughfare, Queen Street.

Here, new stone buildings were going up alongside places like O'Byrne's, a three-decker wood and iron pub with a corrugated iron sun canopy over the paving and iron balconies above. There were new stores alongside old-type colonial shops, and there were betting shops, owned by ready-money bookmakers. Standing in the doorway of one of these betting shops one faced a huge blackboard with the prices of the horses running that day or the next on one of the two racetracks. Next to a betting shop would be a lottery kiosk—there were hundreds of these. Everyone in Brisbane, it seemed, gambled on something.

Behind Queen Street was a street I came to know very well. Here, in a large upper-floor room every evening, the illegal two-up parties began. It was a week or so before my friend Hart took me to the two-up, for first I had to find a job, writing invoices in a shipping office.

"Don't do anything but watch," said Hart at the two-up. "Just sit by me, or stand behind me, and watch how I bet. It's like racing. If your system is sound and you know something, you must win."

We came in the gathering dusk to a doorway beside which two men stood. One recognised Hart, and we were passed inside. On the first floor was the two-up room, most of which was occupied by a square of canvas surrounded by forms and chairs. One man had an armchair. Some thirty men sat around the ringside with silver and notes on the floor at their feet.

In front of the chairman in the armchair was a little pile of notes as well as separate heaps of silver, and in the centre of the ring was the man who was throwing the main. He spun his two pennies off a piece of wood. If they both came heads he won, if they both came tails, he lost, and if they came one of each he spun again. When he lost, the man in the seat to his left threw the main, giving the chairman his money to stake for him.

Hart watched for some time. Some men always backed heads, the others always tails. Hart was deciding whether this was a heads night or a tails night, and this he did by watching the man who owned the joint. If the game was crooked, he would be in it. Eventually, Hart started to back tails. At four in the morning we left. There was a coffee stall open, and we had pies and coffee before starting the long winding walk past the station and up the hill. I asked Hart tentatively how things had gone.

"We lost a bit," he said. "You have to face that, you know. It's all a simple matter of averages."

"I see." I said. "Yes, I suppose it is." I didn't ask how much we had lost, and whether by "we" he meant what was left of my money. Jack was a difficult person to ask a question like that. Hugh could have asked him, because Hugh was a big, lusty, outgoing, forthright chap who would just ask anyone anything. Ted would have asked him too—Ted, the little Cockney mechanic with a grudge against the world. Oh, Ted would certainly have wanted to know what was happening to his money. But Hugh and Ted were not in Brisbane. They had taken a job up country, at some place in the west.

I would have liked to ask Hart, while we munched our pies, whether he was making a lot of money out of racing and two-up, and how much of my money he had. But I put it off, and we went home up the hill to the maze of cheek-by-jowl bungalows where Brisbane lived.

We went to the two-up school whenever we had money. We went to Albion Creek for the racing on Saturdays, and we tried some evening racing at Woolloongabba. Woolloongabba was a five-furlong oval track, where every Monday night there was an "unregistered" race meeting. Owners, trainers, jockeys, officials, bookmakers, everyone who was "unregistered" came here. All those warned off the "registered" turf for one reason or another collected at the 'Gabba, for here they were welcome. It was the spielers' private party.

The small track was lit by arc lamps on high posts about a hundred yards apart, so that the horses flashed through pools of light and vanished into tunnels of darkness. Every horse seemed to be odds on, no matter what one wished to back, and the star lodger where we lived said this was because after the owners had agreed among themselves whose turn it was to win, they double-crossed each other and were liable to be themselves double-crossed by their own jockeys, always bearing in mind that the trainers might have cooked the job among themselves. Hart reluctantly agreed that in the circumstances even he could not hope to win here. The matter of averages could not work out.

We lost all my money. Each Saturday we collected our wages and started on the trail of a fortune once more. Sometimes things went well. The heads came up for us one night and the tails beat us the next. Often, we were completely broke as early as Tuesday night, and our supper on the way home had to be a dozen bananas, which cost twopence—or a penny if one accepted over-ripe ones. It was all going to come out right when the averages had had time.

"There must be different laws in this country from those at home," I said to Hart, "otherwise the bookmakers' shops and the two-up schools and the dice parlours couldn't operate."

"Most people think it's all legal," he said. "We may know better after the Brisbane council election."

This meant nothing to me, even when it came. "Wowsers In" said the newspapers. A wowser was a reformer, a radical or a religious man. But Brisbane life went on just the same. In the two-up school I noticed the escape route was ready —a ladder leading to another roof. And there was an extra man on the door, about thirty yards away. Nothing else was changed.

But one evening when I came back from my work, Hart was waiting for me.

"Pack," he said. "We're getting out on the night train west."

"But Jack," I said, "we're broke!"

"I've collected some money owing," he said, and almost smiled. "It's about time we moved. This place is a bit too hard."

A hundred miles west he said: "The Brisbane gaols will be full tonight. The police have secret orders to raid all the two-up schools, the hazards parlours, the bookies' shops and the brothels. No more Sunday afternoon two-up down by the river. Every pub will be watched. The selling of lottery tickets will be declared illegal. Brisbane is going to be respectable."

"And that's why we're leaving?"

"What was there to stay for?"

"But why in such a hurry?"

He was silent for a few moments and then said: "I thought it would be just as well if I were not on the spot at the time."

"Do they know—the people in the Police Department—do they know you've left, Jack?" But Jack was asleep.

I HAD PLENTY of time for reflection during the long, cold night as the train climbed slowly round the hillsides of Toowoomba. For the first time since I had left home I was lonely. The man opposite was not a friend, nor had Joe Bloom become a friend. Even though, with each in turn, we had desperate moments, we were never together and I had no solace nor encouragement in the company of either. Jack's gambling had fascinated me, but I had had many tormented nights. The strict Methodist upbringing had planted one ineradicable mark upon me—a blazing conscience.

When I watched bookies and listened to their guttural declaiming, they reminded me of the old Dad standing on a street corner in the light of a lamp on a pole, talking socialism, liberalism, Lloyd George, the wickedness of sinners in our midst and, with a heavenly light in his eyes, the glory of Heaven. Dad had ambitions. He wanted to be a councillor, a member of parliament, a parson. But his vocal chords gave trouble and his voice faded. That, as he would say, was his cross.

My ambition was to make money and see my parents live in the luxury of the countryside. I had already lost time, lost the money I had made. Not that the money seemed so important. Even the life in Brisbane, though I was shocked by my own complete failure to make a stand against it, had not left too deep a mark, for I felt I was a witness of it all rather than a participant. My regrets about Brisbane were centred in the fact that it was a disappointing entrance to the state in which, according to Snowy the cook, I might make my fortune. As I looked across at Hart sleeping peacefully, I knew he was no friend for me. The future no longer looked rosy; the bush did not beckon. In short, I was miserable. I needed a friend.

CHAPTER FOUR
A bush wedding

NOW WE WERE going to Roma, Queen City of the West. I had no money and not the faintest idea what lay ahead. Yet there was something about Australia, hard though life could be, which created an aura of plenty. It was impossible to believe one could be hungry or cold here. The piercing sunshine and the bounty of nature were an unwritten promise that one would always live through it.

I had read in a brochure in England that the Queensland government would give a man a hundred and sixty acres of land, freehold and free of charge, with a bonus of ten pounds an acre as he cleared and planted it. I asked Snowy the cook about this back during the burr-cutting which seemed so long ago, and Snowy had said:

"That land is pear country. You seen pear? It's cactus. Put a piece on that barbed wire fence and it'll grow. Sometimes I seen it grow straight up like a forest of trees and so close you couldn't walk through it. Sometimes I seen it thicken out maybe eight feet high, so dense you can't get your axe underneath to cut it. I seen 'em burn it all off with hundreds of gallons of kerosene, and next year it's all up again. The birds eat the pear fruit. Like a tomato inside, full of seed. Emus carry it hundreds of miles and drop it, all fertilised. Pear, Bluey! It'll kill 'Stralia—choke it to death. Ten pound an acre! God strike me bloody pink. God spare me days . . ."

There was no pear, he said, in the sugar country. But that was north, in the coast belt, and I was going west, to the sheeplands.

ROMA was a bush town, built in squares with a pub on each corner, all the town on the south side of the single line rail track, with one main street in which were half a dozen stores, saddlers, and larger pubs. The street was a

29

real street for two or three hundred yards. Then it became a track leading out of the town like any other track.

We booked in at the "Railway", the pub which was the headquarters of Hugh and Ted, and the day we arrived Hart walked into Roma's chief store and got himself the job of office manager, accountant, bookkeeper and financial adviser. No credentials, no proof, nothing to show. He talked a little—he never said very much—and they gave him the job.

He showed me round the store the following day, with the dignity of the owner escorting visiting royalty, and introduced me to various assistants. Hart was warming the situation for me, though this did not occur to me at the time. I was absurdly dense, or childishly innocent, about the motives of Hart.

The store supplied every sheep station and cockatoo farmer within fifty or a hundred miles with literally everything needed, from wire and sheep dip to new dresses for the squatter's wife. Women's hats were heaped in a cardboard box standing on a sack of potatoes. In one corner was an open barrel of English dried, salted herrings—soldiers, we called them in my London suburb.

Sacks of maize, heaps of harness, shelves of tobacco in tins and in cakes, bolts of cloth, men's hats, men's dungarees, grey flannel singlets, elastic-sided boots for boundary riders, billycans, waterbags, canned meat, canned herrings with a Leadenhall Street label, bales of fencing wire, shovels and a small quantity of very expensive cabbages: these were the hot selling lines of the big store of Roma.

Around the blocks were the residences of the Roma people—mostly small bungalows, with large verandahs, children playing in dusty yards. The pubs opened sharp at six every morning and remained open continuously, business or no business, until three o'clock the next morning. At the "Railway" they charged us a pound a week each for our beds and all the meat we could eat three times a day with an egg thrown in on Sunday mornings.

The "Railway" faced the rail track. It stood, inevitably, on a corner, and on the other corner was the "Royal".

During the hot afternoon men drifted along and formed a ring in the middle of the road between the two pubs, a chairman took charge and a game of two-up started.

The advantage of siting the game there, observed Hart, was that the cops could be seen approaching from any direction. When a cop appeared, there was time to finish the toss, settle up, and amble into the pub. Every man put a shilling into the pool and had a shake of the dice. The winner took the lot and paid for drinks all round, including the publican and the cop. This place being a railway town, everything in the bar was sixpence.

At the weekend Hugh and Ted came in. Hugh swept us all into the bar for drinks, called for two pints for himself and drank the lot without a pause except to change pots. Ted, I fancied, was glad to see me.

"Thought you'd a gone home," he said. This was his grudging acknowledgment of the fact that I hadn't. I told him Mr Bloom had said he would go back.

"Who, Bloom?" said Ted, derisively. "He won't go back. Bloom will go on cursin' this bleedin' country, gettin' drunk, shiftin' around until he settles into something he likes, and there he'll stay. Bloom likes his beer too much to go back."

Hugh and Ted were sinking a bore for water twenty miles out, earning good money. I listened to their stories of their job, and their camp and their food, and was dismally aware that I was the odd man out, with nothing in my pocket and no job.

That day a party of farming folk came in to stay at the "Railway", including two families. A boy of sixteen of one family was being married to a girl of fourteen of the other. They were all full of liquor by six o'clock, when the married pair went up to bed. There was a piano. Frost, the publican, desperately afraid of losing good customers, said to the four of us Englishmen: "Can one of youse blokes play the piano?"

The bush was full of pubs with pianos with no one able to play them.

"No use to me," said Hugh. Jack shook his head. Ted

said: "I'll sing for them if someone can play."

I said: "I can play a bit. Not much."

"All you can drink," said the publican, leading me to the piano. "Here he is," he announced. "All the way from the Old Country just to play fer youse.'

"Tell me what youse want me to play for youse," I said, in my best Australian.

These people, who had lived in the bush all their lives, and whose offspring (now locked in wedded bliss) had never before seen a train, had progressed no farther, musically, than "Blue Bells of Scotland" and "Goodbye, Dolly Gray". These songs, and a few more, they sang and jigged to, as pint after pint of beer was sent across and stood on the piano top for me. Everyone in the pub wanted to buy the piano player a beer. Fortunately, Hugh was at hand to demolish most of it.

And then Ted insisted on singing. He knew all the Harry Champion songs, every word of every verse, and he told me he would start with "Any Old Iron". I staggered through the tunes hour after hour. Harry Champion was followed by Gus Elen, after which Ted switched to old English ballads. He had a deep, nasal, penetrating voice with grit in it, and he used it with intense feeling. When Ted sang, by God he sang.

The publican was delighted. At three in the morning he shoved the farming folk into their bedrooms and closed the pub. To me he said: "No need to look fer a job, Bluey. Yer fixed. Pound a week and yer keep and all the beer youse can drink. Just go on playin' that old joanna, and when things are slack you can teach my daughter, Gert."

Hugh and Ted went back to their bore-sinking and Hart went off, looking very smart and very English, to the big store, and to his desk behind the sweet potatoes and boxes of women's underclothes. I went to the station to see the train come in, and most of the population of Roma was there too.

It came, only an hour late, amid a hubbub of greetings and laughter. The driver climbed down from his cab and disappeared across the track towards the "Railway". Goods were hauled off, buggies and wagons loaded up. A town-dressed man and his wife were met by the buggy from the big hotel down by the store and were driven off, followed by the stares of the womenfolk.

I helped myself to a mug of water from the swinging waterbag in the shade, and standing by were a group of men to whom a man with thick, powerful arms said: "Any of youse blokes want a job?"

"What job?" one asked.

"Sleeper work on the line, hundred and fifty miles west."

One by one they smiled and turned away.

"I'd like the job," I said.

The ganger sized me, critically. "It's heavy work," he said. "Sleepers is heavy work."

"Too right, Dan," said one of the crowd. "Heavy and hot. Only bloody hot."

"I could try," I said.

He shrugged. "You could. I shall fire you if you fall down on it. You work in pairs and a man don't like a partner that can't do his whack. Get aboard this train. She goes in ten minutes."

I had asked for it. I ran over to the pub, wondering what sort of fool I was to take on a job too tough and hot for Australians who had worked hard in the tropical sun all their lives. And as I entered the hotel I met Gert, a big, unkempt blonde of thirty or forty.

"Time for me pianner lesson, Bluey," she said.

I packed my swag and fled for the train.

We reached the small line of mice-infested tents that night and the train pulled up for us to get off. The ganger issued me with some food, and next morning we all piled on two pumpers and chased emus along the line for a couple of miles. This was the scene of operations. I was given a partner, a pick, a crowbar and a sledge-hammer, and the idea was conveyed to me in simple terms that we merely clawed the flints away from the old sleeper, pulled out the steel dogs, hauled the old sleeper out and replaced it in reverse with a new one.

The work was so heavy, the heat reflected by the rails

so piercingly hot, that by afternoon smoko the ganger very properly fired me. I was all but dead, my sweaty pants clinging to me, the crowbar so burning that I could not hold it and my partner so angry by the fact that we were ten sleepers behind the rate for the time, that I was relieved when the ganger said: "I'll take over, Bluey. Get back to camp and I'll pay you off tonight."

I staggered slowly back along the rail track, my head on my chest, and all but trod on a silver snake, eight feet long, stretched plumb across the rails. I screamed as I jumped back, and eventually drove it off into a culvert by slinging rocks at it.

The ganger paid me six shillings less one and eightpence for food, and before the pumpers left next morning he put out a flag for the next train to stop. One came along during the day. It was a goods train, going still farther west, out to Charleville and beyond, to the farthest point of the line, where the Cunnamulla extension was being built.

"How far?" asked the guard.

"I don't know," I said.

"Looking fer work?"

"Yes. But I'm afraid I can't do sleepers."

He gave me half his meal and commented, "Don't seem your sort of life out here. Got to be tough and strong, and used to the heat and the flies. But you might find something out on the Cunnamulla extension."

CHAPTER FIVE
The big steal

WE TRAVELLED west all through the night, and next morning we stopped in the middle of nowhere. Three men were working, putting up some fencing alongside the recently built line. There was wire to unload. I jumped down and helped a friendly, handsome young Australian whose eyes were crinkly with fun and good humour, so that I had no difficulty in saying: "No chance of any work around here, I don't suppose?"

"Well, now," he said. "Hey, Dutch!"

Dutch, whose hair was going grey, came over.

"Cove here wants a job."

He looked at me keenly, the way they all did in the bush, as though probing my soul as well as my muscles.

"We're on contract," he said. "Not a good one, kid."

"You don't have to pay me," I said eagerly. "It looks fine here, among these shady trees, and I'll soon learn about fencing. Besides, I can make bread . . ."

"You can bake bread?" said the smiling one. "Hey, Carlo! Cove here can bake bread! Dutch, let's take him in."

Now Carlo came over, the dark one from Victoria. "I'm wantin' some good cookin', Dutch," he said. "Man can't work without good cookin'."

Dutch wavered. "You're in," he said.

I grabbed my bag and jumped off the train. "All the best," said the guard. "These are good blokes, or I wouldn't leave you stay here." The driver tooted with his whistle a happy farewell, and I dumped my swag among the red ironbark and mulga trees and felt this was a grand country if you could take it.

They showed me the camp, half a mile back in the scrub, and I stirred the fire, got it cracking with some hefty logs, and found the flour and the soda and salt, and started to bake some damper. It was hot and just right when the three men came in at sundown. One had some fish caught in a creek, and these we toasted on twigs and ate out of our hands.

They were three of the finest, frankest, most friendly men I had seen in my life, all with bulging muscles like weight-lifters. Carlo had an accordion, and played and sang old bush songs as we sat around the camp fire, with Dutch, the fortyish, grey-haired one, joining in, and Frank of the ready grin just smoking and enjoying it all. Carlo passed me his plug of Yankee Doodle, but although I had been a year in the country and regarded myself as practically Australian, chewing Yankee Doodle was still away beyond the ability of my tender stomach.

They asked me no questions about myself and when I lay under a bush that night, I felt immensely happy, and proud to have been accepted into the circle of three men who were all firm friends, with clear eyes, frank open faces and a love of music. Half an hour before dawn each one rolled over, relit what was left of the previous night's pungent pipe ashes, and went to wash while I got busy with the breakfast. My job was to cook, to bring coffee or tea for "smoko" and to help with the wiring when I had time. It could be I was making a better start on my fortune.

I learned a great deal. They caught or shot jack rabbits, kangaroo rats, fish, and these I had to skin or gut and cook. I learned to split posts and strain the wires with a horse. In short spells I attacked the crowbar again. They all seemed to like me, and the only thing I did not understand was that on Sundays, when no work was done, all three washed their clothes, as is the custom in the bush, and then very nicely said goodbye and disappeared for the day. They never said, on their return, where they had been, and they brought back nothing for the pot.

One night we got to talking about the job.

"We made a bad contract, Bluey," said Dutch. "We get twenty-two pound a mile for this fencing, and it wasn't bad, so far as I could tell, until we struck red rock. Making two-foot post holes in rock can't be done at that price. We work dawn till sundown, as you know, six days a week, and when

I want to draw some advance they tell us they ain't none. It's this figuring, Bluey."

"Figuring?"

"Yair. We get so much a hundred for post splitting and so much for unloading by the ton and so much for the horse drawing the wires through the strainers. Then there's the stores account. Frank smokes a lot more than we do and I paid for the tent. That's the sort of figuring that licks us. We can write our names and that's all."

"Well," I said, "I'll do the accounts. I can do that stuff on my head."

I wrote to Ted and was almost poetic on bush comradeship. Rashly, I told him we should all do pretty well out of it when I had figured things out. The contract, however, was a bad one. I had to tell my new friends we weren't doing any good at all. In fact, after paying for our stores we seemed to be working for less than nothing.

Dutch wasn't greatly upset by this news, but they resorted to sawing a foot off each post to make the crowbar work easier, until the inspector came along and pulled up a couple of posts and warned us he wouldn't pay for the work at all if it happened again. But the trio weren't distressed. They went on working hard—not desperately hard, but hard, because it was the only way they knew, and every Sunday they disappeared for the day and returned about sundown, all smiling.

I felt I had three fine friends. True, they shut me out one night when they went a bit away from the camp fire and had a discussion in low tones. I felt it was none of my business and moved farther away, perhaps ostentatiously. On the following Sunday, they were away from dawn, without waiting for breakfast, and when they came back at sundown, very happy, I said: "I have the accounts right up to date."

"What do they say?" asked Dutch.

"It's getting worse," I said apologetically. "I don't mind for myself. It's decent of you to have me here at all. But it's pretty crook for you blokes doing all that work for nothing."

Nobody seemed distressed. "We always knew it was a

lousy contract," said Frank, with a grin.

"Who the hell cares," said Carlo.

"So long as we eat," added Dutch.

"Too right," laughed Frank.

"That reminds me. I must have a new shirt and pants," said Carlo. "Get 'em on the next order, Bluey."

"We'll all have new shirt and pants," said Dutch. "You, too, Bluey."

"What, me?"

"Too right," said Frank. "You're a partner, Bluey. Full partner."

And then one Sunday, following a Saturday evening in which Carlo played his accordion for us for hours, they shook me early. I dressed, and we all hurried away through the scrub in the semi-darkness with some bread and cold meat to eat on the way. Through timber, through scrub, across plain, over a running creek, into another belt of mulga we went, and at length came to quite a small creek.

It was dry, but half a mile further along there was a large billabong, full of good, clear water. We approached very quietly, and I noticed that the earth at the further side of the pool was churned as though by many hooves. I felt the thrill of the big game hunter, though I had no clue what we were hunting. We lay on our stomachs, whispering. After more than an hour Dutch put his ear to the ground, and gave a signal. We lay stock still.

Presently the quarry came—a great mob of horses, with foals cavorting around their mothers, and sturdy two-year-olds, colts and fillies and mares in foal. There were hundreds of horses. All seemed to me to be the hack type, for saddle or light harness—roans, bays and browns. My friends scrutinised them horse by horse, and after an hour, the mob suddenly flung away. The tension eased, we stretched ourselves and settled down to eat our bread and meat.

Dutch selected a stick and started to whittle it. "You see, Bluey," he said, "we're horse men. I been a cattle drover on and off for thirty years. Carlo was wellnigh born on a horse, and so was Frank."

"Too right," said Frank, smiling easily.

"They don't pay money for horse men today. Pound a week and rough tucker for boundary riding, mostly pulling ewes outer ditches. Thirty bob fer cutting out cattle. And here's me and Carlo and Frank has to get stuck into a fencing contract."

I thought hard for appropriate words. There was a short silence. Carlo said, with unexpected force: "Me! I kin ride the roughest, toughest brumby foaled. And I have to dig post holes!" His dark eyes flashed fire.

I oozed sympathy and admiration. "So you come here every Sunday to see horses, because you love horses."

"You bet," said Dutch.

Dutch whittled the sliver with care until it was thin and sharp. He began to talk deliberately and slowly, as we others watched the pointing of the barb.

"I was born in what is now Rhodesia," he said. He seemed to be talking to me, in particular, but also to himself.

"There were no fences and no grazing rights. There were no shooting rights. A man branded his own stock, just as he does in any other country, but any animal more than half grown and not branded belonged to the veldt, like the lions and the antelope. Many horses ran wild and bred, and still do. And any man who takes them and brands them is the owner. Is that right?"

"There's wild ponies on Dartmoor at home," I said. "I've heard they don't belong to anyone."

"It's natural law," said Dutch. "You can only live in such places as Rhodesia and here in the backblocks of Queensland by natural law. There ain't any police, no soldiers, no judges out here. Only a cop and a magistrate in the small townships. Politicians think they can make laws down in the cities which give the big squatters the power of life and death over everything that runs or flies. Men who have never set foot in Australia profit from the land we're settin' on this minute, and in law we're not allowed to knock over a jack rabbit or hook a yellowbelly out of that crick."

Carlo's eyes flashed as Dutch said these words, and I sensed the heightening feeling. It made me quite angry, too.

"They wouldn't stop me knocking over a jack rabbit if I was hungry," I said belligerently. "I'd kill a sheep, if I had to."

"Sheep," said Dutch quietly, "are always branded. To kill a branded sheep is theft. I don't agree with theft."

Snubbed, I opened my mouth to remonstrate, but thought better of it. My own feelings seemed of no importance at the moment. Dutch was discussing world freedoms, not jack rabbits.

"Suppose," said Dutch, "I had a million acres of scrub. So much scrub I hadn't even fenced it. Suppose my grandfather got the lease for practically nothing, sixty years ago. And suppose a young stallion and mebbe half a dozen mares are running wild, and they settle on a patch of my scrub. Would they belong to me? Yes, if I branded 'em. But suppose I didn't even know they were here?"

The fine eyes of the Rhodesian turned to each member of his audience. No one replied, for they knew, and I knew, that Dutch had decided to reply to his own question. He laid down the sliver and flicked the knife so that it stuck, quivering, in the tree trunk beside him.

"According to natural law," said Dutch, "them horses belong to no man, until they're caught and branded."

"That's so," said Carlo.

"My oath," said Frank.

"Natural law," said Dutch, in level tones, "is the law of all free men in what's left of the open spaces of the world."

He whittled a new stick steadily for a couple of minutes. I waited in silence. Something big was coming.

"There's four hundred young horses in that mob," said Dutch, huskily, nodding towards his left shoulder. "Four hundred horses perduced from one stallion and a few mares running wild. This paddick is mebbe four or five hundred square miles. In law, it is part of Merrunda, but they isn't a single sheep or bullock in the whole paddick, nor probably never has been. Not one of these four hundred horses was ever branded except the old stallion, and his brand isn't the Merrunda brand."

40

"Well, then," I said, excited, "Merrunda doesn't even know they exist! They don't belong to anyone."

"Until someone brands 'em," shouted Carlo.

"Too right," said Frank, smiling widely. "Too right, Bluey, old pal."

"Bluey," said Dutch, "me and Carlo and Frank are horse men. Real horse men are honest. We don't steal. We believe in natural law, not in laws made for city folk. We love horses. Here we find four hundred horses running wild and unbranded, owned by no one. We say it's a sin against nature to leave a horse run wild. The natural life of a horse is to be broken in, taught to work and properly fed and groomed. We're the first to find these horses. By natural law, we claim them."

I was too shaken to think out the implications. "Will they let you?"

Dutch reflected. "It's like a prospector finding gold," he said. "If he strikes gold he registers his claim, and the gold is his to get. If we find wild horses, we brand 'em, and they're our horses. In natural law there's no difference. That's all we're concerned with."

"Bluey," said Carlo, "we're going to take them horses and brand 'em. Then they'll be ours. We're going to drove 'em right across the continent to Adelaide. The trail's nearly two thousand miles, and Dutch and me knows every inch of the way we're going, where to water and where to feed. We'll take mebbe six months, or twelve months, and on the way we'll rig a yard and break in the best of 'em to the saddle. In Adelaide they'll fetch from fifteen to twenty-five or thirty pound apiece."

I did a rapid calculation. Averaged at twenty, it made eight thousand pounds. "By crikey," I said. "That's a fortune."

"Too right," laughed the genial Frank. "It's a lot of beer."

"I know that trail blindfold," said Carlo. His eyes sparked. "There's a full moon on Friday week."

"That," said Dutch, "is when we go."

My thoughts were whirling. This was the biggest thing

I had ever met in my life. It was like meeting a man who had just discovered a gold reef.

"I don't expect you'd take me in?" I said.

"We was thinking," said Dutch, awkwardly. "We ain't none of us educated, like you. There's such things, f'rinstance, as wayleaves. You can't take horses across the state borders without wayleaves, nor you can't sell horses without wayleaves. There's the stores to buy, and cutting up the dough at the sales. Then again, we thought, Bluey's a good pal and he's worked with us on a bad contract and nothing to come bar a new pair of strides and a shirt. Why shouldn't Bluey come along, if he's thinking with us?"

CHAPTER SIX

Charleville is dry!

I WROTE to Ted and said goodbye. I promised him I would come back and find him, and together we would invest my fortune in some enterprise and later on I'd be able to get my old people out to live in comfort and sunshine by the warm sea.

Why I should make Ted this offer I could not have explained. I told him of the fine character of my new friends, and mentioned that if one's conscience was satisfied that a thing was morally right, that was what really mattered. I didn't cross-examine myself about this. Dutch couldn't do anything wrong. His logic was sound. It was just that Ted had a suspicious nature.

On the Wednesday night before full moon we went into conference. Dutch explained the plans. "Bluey," he said, "we agree that you're to hold the money, but you only spend it as we all vote. Here's all our dough—fifty-two pound."

"I've got a money belt," I said. "See. I'll put it away now." I pulled off my shirt and stuffed the notes and gold into the pockets of the belt around my waist. My fingers were trembling slightly. It was a great deal of money.

"Tomorrow," said Dutch, "we'll buy our stores. Flour, sugar, tobacco and what else. We won't stay in the town. After dusk we'll pull out and camp for a bit. Then, when the moon's up, we'll show you the trail to take with the buggy, and later on, mebbe a day or so, we'll be alongside with the horses."

"Do we have to wait in Charleville until dusk?" I asked.

"You bet we do," said Carlo. "We got to get them way-leaves, don't we, Frank?"

Frank burst into laughter.

Early on the Thursday morning Dutch put his horses into the buggy and we struck camp, and drove towards Charleville. I was alive to my new importance as an educated man, and asked for facts about wayleaves.

"Yair," said Dutch. "Very important, the wayleaves."

"We'll get 'em tomorrow night," said Frank. "The office is only a wood hut."

"It's a question," said Dutch, "of stamping and signing the forms correctly. I seen wayleaves often enough but how they're fixed I don't know. I reckon you'll do that righto, Bluey. Then we get the saddle horses. Frank's got two and Carlo's got one. I'll ride Frank's pack horse and you'll drive the buggy. We'll get along."

"You bet," said Carlo.

Carlo played his accordion and we all sang, even Frank, who couldn't really sing at all.

In the late afternoon, we pulled up in the dusty main street of Charleville. I felt like one of the musketeers. A great adventure was about to start.

"Must have a pint," said Frank, unnecessarily.

We walked into a bar.

"Four pints," said Frank.

It was dry, dusty and hot in Charleville.

"Just in?" asked the man behind the bar.

Frank nodded.

"Then you wouldn't know. There's no beer."

The three men gaped incredulously. "No beer?" said Dutch, harshly. "What's the joke?"

"No joke," said the hotel man. "My bloody oath. No joke, pal. The town's dry. There ain't a drop of beer in Charleville." He swatted a bunch of flies on the bar counter. "Hasn't happened these twenty years. Bin no beer for a week."

"Let's go to the Palace," said Carlo, making for the door. Beer had suddenly become considerably more than urgent.

"No beer there," said the man behind the bar. "I wouldn't kid you. The town's drunk dry."

I hesitated to ask for a soft drink. Beer was so obviously important to my friends.

Frank looked at Carlo is dismay.

Dutch made a swift decision: "Gimme whisky."

44

"Yair," said Carlo. "Whisky."

Frank nodded.

"No whisky," said the hotel man, patiently. "Don't youse blokes understand? Charleville's dry. Bone dry. No draught, no bottled beer, no whisky, no schnapps, no brandy, no rum. People are practically dyin' of thirst. Ain't a drink in Charleville till the train comes up tomorrow."

"Struth," muttered Carlo. "It jess don't make sense."

"Too right it don't," said Frank.

Dutch's face darkened with gathering fury. He started to swear violently. I shrank away to one end of the bar, bewildered. I had never realised beer could mean so much to people who weren't soaks. For myself, a ginger beer off the ice would have been heaven if one could have asked for it without acknowledging one was only a kid.

"It's no good cursing," said the publican, firmly. "Ain't my fault. Ain't anyone's fault. It's bin pretty bloody hot about here. We can't keep beer long, y'know." He looked from one to the other. They were like starving men robbed of a cooked and fragrant dinner. "You fellers come far?" he asked, with sympathy.

"We haven't had a drink between us for five months," said Carlo. "Five months out on the Cunnamulla extension, working twelve hours a day, hotter'n hell." He licked his lips.

Frank stared at the empty shelves. "Nothin' at all? Not a bottle of—I'd even drink port wine. Any muck with a kick in it."

The publican wavered and then said: "Listen, you blokes want a drink bad. I got some booze, but it's lousy stuff. I don't recommend it, I warn you."

"Bring it," snarled Dutch.

The publican left the bar and came back with six green, narrow-necked bottles. He put them on the bar counter.

"It's French," he said. "They call it Starboard Light in Sydney but its proper name is Cream dee Menth. I must've been drunk when I bought it from a traveller. It's sweet as molasses."

"I seen it once in Melbourne," said Carlo. "A girl's

drink."

"I'm for giving it a run," said Frank. "Does it fizz?"

"I'll take a pint," said Dutch. "Bluey, pay him for the six bottles."

"You can't drink this stuff like it was beer," warned the man behind the bar. He pushed four half-pint glasses across the bar counter and drew the corks. "It's lousy booze, boys, but it's got a kick."

"We split fair," said Dutch, filling four glasses. "Christ, I could drink liquid cyanide. You want a drink?"

The publican shook his head. "I'll wait fer the beer."

"Here's a go," said Dutch and swallowed the liqueur.

He looked at the empty glass and frowned. "Mighty sweet, eh?"

"I didn't taste nothin'," said Carlo. "Too dusty inside, I reckon."

"Nor me," said Frank. "Let's give it another go."

Dutch filled up the three glasses. "How 'bout you, Bluey?"

I liked the peppermint flavour but found the liqueur difficult to encompass quickly. Still, I felt I wasn't doing my stuff by my pals and jerked some more into my stomach. Dutch filled his glass.

"Here's a go," said Dutch and sank the second glass.

Already the need for booze was less urgent.

"I'd still go fer a pint of beer," said Carlo, a trifle thickly, pushing his emptied glass away.

"That's me," said Frank.

For myself, static objects were already less static. Definitions faded. My stomach was hot.

Dutch grabbed three bottles in one huge fist and his glass in the other. "Come over here, kid," he said confidentially. I was glad to sit down at the small table.

"Let's go find some beer," said Carlo to Frank.

The third half-pint acted pretty fast on Dutch, though I was beyond accurate observation. I felt queer, very queer. "Where's Carlo and Frank?" I asked.

"They'll come back,' said Dutch, breathing heavily. "You got the dough, ain't you?"

46

I felt the bulge beneath my shirt. "I've got it."

"Okay. They'll come back," said Dutch. "You got all our dough, kid. We trust you, kid. That's why we took you along. Them other two's good horse men, Bluey. My oath. I can handle 'em. You ain't drinking nothing. Good horse men can take their booze, kid. This French muck wouldn't make a cat drunk."

The publican looked in.

"Whaddya want?" snarled Dutch, suddenly angry.

"Don't get funny," warned the publican. "I said to go slow on that stuff."

"Get out," said Dutch. His face was dark with alcoholic storm.

"That kid," said the publican. "He don't want any more booze. Come and have some grub, kid."

"Good idea," I mumbled, and attempted to stand.

Dutch shoved me back into my chair and grabbed an empty bottle by the neck. The liqueur had bitten deep into his brain, and its sweetness was torturing his palate. Menacingly, he got up, lurched towards the bar and flung the bottle. Rows of smashed glasses and mirrors crashed to the floor. The publican came swiftly round the bar counter and found himself in a powerful grip.

The contest was all over within a minute. The drunken bushman hurled him bodily across the room, where his head struck the corner of a table. Dutch reeled back, swallowed a full glass of the booze, and staggered through the swing doors into the dusk.

A few minutes later, Frank and Carlo came back and surveyed the scene. Frank turned my sozzled frame gently, slung me easily over his broad shoulders, and also went forth into the night. Wild shouting could be heard to the right. Frank and Carlo turned to the left. I knew no more.

THE HOTEL MAN was cleaning up his bar next morning when I entered.

"I thought you was dead," said the publican. "You look like you was. Where did you get that thing?"

"Pardon me," I said, "I should be very grateful if you

would tell me where my pals are. This is my pal Carlo's accordion. He'll be worrying about it."

The hotel man looked at me shrewdly. "Seems you all got screwed up last night on that Cream dee Menth. One of 'em got to smashing up the bar. Then he started smashing up the town. He's in the gaol."

"Which one?"

"Feller you called Dutch. The others—I don't know. They ain't in town no more. Mebbe you better go round to the gaol and see your pal. Tell him from me," the publican added pleasantly, "I hope he gets ten years."

The gaol was a one-room bungalow divided into three cells. It stood at the back of the police sergeant's house. Nearby, for convenience, was the domestic woodpile. Dutch was half asleep on a blanket on the floor of his cell. The man who had been so much a man in the bush glared with savage, bloodshot eyes at the pale, freckled face darkening the barred cube in the cell door. The cell stank horridly. Dutch pushed the streaks of grey hair from his forehead.

"Hello, Dutch," I said.

"Hello, kid," said Dutch. "What's the news?"

"I can't find Frank and Carlo," I said miserably.

"Oh, them. Don't worry about them."

"Dutch. I've got some awful bad news. I must have got drunk last night. I've lost the money, Dutch."

"That's all right, kid,' said Dutch. "I reckon you didn't lose no money. Them thieves took it. Frank and Carlo's got it. Sure thing. Frank, I'd say. He'd steal from his mother."

I listened without understanding.

"It was taken from my belt, too. I woke up in a China-man's cabbage patch outside the town."

"That'll be Frank," said Dutch.

"It's queer," I said. "Whoever robbed me left two pounds in my belt and this." I produced a cake of tobacco.

Dutch hauled himself to his feet, took the plug and smelt it. "Frank's," he said. "This is for me to chew. He knew I'd get six months. He's probably stolen my buggy, too. But I'll

48

catch up with him. It's a mighty small continent for people like us."

"Six months!" There was so much I didn't understand. I offered the pound notes. "Will you take the money?"

"That's meant for you, kid," said Dutch. He swore softly and deliberately to himself. "So they strip me clean, and send me a plug of the worst tobacco in Australia. And two quid for the boy. But it's a small country, by God. A small country. My bloody oath."

I hadn't finished. I held up Carlo's glittering accordion. "There's another thing. By my side in the cabbage patch was this. It's Carlo's. What shall I do with it? I must find Carlo, Dutch, mustn't I?"

Dutch was at last perplexed. "Strike me hooray," he said. "Did the dago give you that?"

"He was awfully fond of it," I said. "Why should he give it to me? Dutch, where are they? When will they come back? When do we start to get the horses?"

Through the bars, the bushman could see my tears.

"If they'd been some beer in the town," he muttered, "it would have been a bosker." But I think he knew it never would have been. I think he had always known, though refusing to acknowledge to himself, that the first contact with booze would smash everything. Life had perhaps been that way for a good many years. It was an old and familiar story in the bush.

"Out there in camp," he said quietly, half to himself, "things looked different. They always do, in the bush. A man shares his grub with a stranger. A man gets ideas about things, too. Who should own what, and all that stuff. In town, nobody shares. If you get drunk, they steal your dough. Then they kick you out. Bluey, it was a good idea, but it wouldn't have worked. We'd have got ten years apiece for stealing them horses. It didn't seem like stealing then, but it does now, Bluey. There's police law in Charleville."

"I don't think it was stealing," I said. It was a good effort but unconvincing.

"No," said Dutch, "but we knew it was, and we knew

49

you didn't. Funny thing, we all liked you. Nice clean kid among a bunch of bush crooks tryin' to pretend. Mebbe it's as well I soaked up that green poison. Listen, Bluey: there ain't no room for Ned Kelly in the bush today. You get down the line to your pal."

I walked out of the police sergeant's yard still not entirely in my full senses but acutely aware that, whereas the day before I had just about everything, on this morning I had lost it all. The horses, the excitement, the long drive, the money, all these I could bear to lose. But I had also lost my friends, and in a faith-shattering way.

The genial, handsome Frank, for whom everything was good-oh, bonzer or too right. The ever-smiling, helpful Frank who had been first to invite me into the foursome. Easy-going, hard-working Frank, who asked little but comradeship. Could Frank be a bush crook, a double-crosser?

Carlo, ah! Carlo I had never understood. He accepted me and appreciated my soda bread, as he might have appreciated a new, strong horse for pulling the top wires through the posts. Why then, the priceless accordion? Because he knew I had envied it, coveted it more than anything I had ever seen? But he, too, loved it. Was it a pay-off, a recompense, or did he feel guilty about me? Did such men ever feel guilty about anything? This I doubted very strongly. There is no guilt in the bush.

And Dutch. That fine, strong character, with his wonderful sentiments, his powers of leadership and planning, his years of experience and his knowledge of the bush world and traps. Seeing Dutch on the floor of that cell, his face grimy and haggard, his greying hair streaked wildly, his eyes dulled with senseless drinking, this was my greatest shock.

In all my life, even in schooldays, I had never had a friend who was more than a friendly acquaintance, until I met Dutch, and in him, until this moment, I would have confided my innermost secrets. Only Dutch could have persuaded me that the venture with the horses out at Merrunda was honourable. What doubts may have begun to hatch in my mind had been immediately smothered by the overwhelming belief that Dutch would do nothing wrong.

Charleville was normal. The beer had arrived, the saloons were all open and full. Men were getting drunk at nine in the morning. If the full moon had been a day later, what then? There was that queer talk of wayleaves. Would I have suspected then? Or would it have been too late to turn back? They had told me, over the camp fire, of great "droves" over the route to Adelaide from Central Queensland, with cattle and horses. Prices were better there than on the Queensland coast, they said.

"No room for Ned Kelly in the bush today," Dutch had said. Strange that, for it was a play called "Ned Kelly, the Bushranger", at the Collins Theatre, Islington, which I had seen as a boy and which first inspired my ambition to come to this country. Ned Kelly, I recalled, was a nice-looking man—that is, the Ned Kelly at the Collins—but he was killed by a police bullet. Dutch would have been an outlaw fifty years before.

CHAPTER SEVEN

Five pounds or fifteen days

I WAS NOT YET finished with Charleville. In the yards outside the station a sheep train was being loaded. I put down my swag and Carlo's shining accordion and offered to help. It was already hot.

"Whack in, kid," said one. "You want a ride down?"

"Well, yes, I do," I said. We worked steadily through the dust and the heat until evening, when the last of the sheep were sent scuttering noisily up the wooden slope into the double-decker wagon. It was a long train of sheep wagons with a solitary compartment for the sheepherders on the end of the last coach. No guard was carried, since there were no signals on this single line.

We climbed into the narrow compartment and sank into the seats, exhausted. One man said: "We've earned a drink" and produced a bottle of whisky and three half-pint tin pannikins, which he half-filled. I sipped the raw spirit gratefully and wiped the sweaty grime from my eyes.

"Time we was moving," said one. "Driver knows we're ready."

There was a toot of the driver's whistle, but at that moment our door was flung open. The stationmaster was there. He was a smallish man with a small moustache, young, important-looking. He held a paper.

"Everything in order," he said, "but"—he dwelt for effect—"this says transport for two men. One of you out!"

The sheep men looked at me. "Tough luck, Bluey," they said.

"You mean I can't ride down?" I said. "After all that work?"

"It's what the little bastard says."

"He wants a poke on the nose."

The stationmaster hesitated, decided not to reply, and waved me out. I clutched my swag and the accordion and climbed down wearily. We were some way outside the station and there were no signals. The stationmaster waved, the driver blew his whistle, and the train began to move slowly.

I was never brave, but at that moment, embittered and chagrined, I had my moment of madness. I placed the accordion under my right arm, the arm holding the swag, and swung my clenched left fist with all the force I could muster as I wheeled into the stationmaster. He fell flat on his back, and I jumped into the moving train and slammed the door.

"That," said my companions, almost in unison, "was a beaut." One handed me my whisky.

But there were things about trains I did not know. Within another hundred yards, the train pulled up. Somehow, the stationmaster had stopped the train. I felt like a live fish in a net, for in the bush it was impossible to run away, impossible to hide. A man must eat and he must have water. Tracks were few and tracks must be followed or you died of thirst. So I waited.

The policeman came eventually, the train pulled away, and I walked through the town, into the police sergeant's yard, past the woodpile, and entered the centre cell where I had seen my great friend Dutch ten hours before. My accordion and my swag were taken away. The cell was a narrow passage, with one thin blanket and a wooden floor to sleep on. Queer noises came from the right and the left, but after half an hour the sergeant appeared.

"The wife," he said, "reckoned you'd had no tea." He handed me a quart of hot, strong, raw tea in a quart tin mug and a couple of pounds of grilled steak on a tin plate, with half a loaf of bread. No knife or fork. No salt. At sun-up, I was pulled out for a wash in the yard and given the axe and shown the woodpile.

"Who are the others?" I asked. "They kick up the strangest row."

One, he said, had the DTs and the other was a bush-mad Asiatic.

"We get 'em all here," said the sergeant, cheerfully, "but I never seen a newchum in the jug before. They tell me you stoushed the little bastard up at the station?"

"S'right," I said, feeling strangely elated.

He shook a warning finger. "You're due in court at ten," he said. "You say you're sorry, you got no dough, you want to see your sick mother down the line, and you get off with a caution. Nobody likes that little bastard up at the station."

In court I was charged with assault. The stationmaster stepped into the witness box. If I had not seen him I would have done exactly as the sergeant advised, but the sight of the stationmaster's black eye was too much for me. It was, in fact, a beaut. I had never dreamt I could deliver such punishment. I forgot that the actual contact of my fist on his eye was the purest fluke. A thrill of ecstasy passed through me.

The magistrate listened coldly to the stationmaster and then turned to the freckly youth with still a hint of the delicate, standing in the dock.

"Anything to say?"

"Nothing," I said.

He was startled. "Nothing?"

"Nothing," I said, recklessly.

He looked at the sergeant in weary, puzzled fashion, then back to me. "Five pounds or fifteen days," he said.

"Prisoner's got a couple of quid, yer honour," said the sergeant.

The magistrate hesitated. "I'll think about it," he said.

So I went back to the cell, with the bush-mad Asiatic and the man with the DTs, and had my quart of raw tea and two pounds of steak three times a day.

"Can't you send a wire to someone?" asked the sergeant's wife. Both she and her husband were horrified that I was remaining in the gaol. I suppose that to them I didn't belong to the gaol fraternity and had no right to be there. I thought I might wire Ted, but eventually thought not. No one else could I really call a friend. Five pounds was a great deal of money.

But news travels fast in the bush and on the third day a railway fireman stationed at Roma and living at the "Railway" came to the police station and paid the fine.

"Why didn't you wire?" he said.

"I didn't know anyone," I said. "Who paid all this money?"

"Your friend Hart."

"Hart!"

"Yes. He went round the bar demanding a dollar from everyone. Then he handed it all to me and said 'Bring him back'. And back you come. Ever ridden on the footplate?"

"What *is* the footplate?"

I went back in triumph, without paying my fare, on the footplate with the driver and the fireman, and despite the stationmaster. My self-esteem, as well as the esteem of all bush people, went up several points, not because I had stoushed the stationmaster but because of the reason: I had upheld the honour of bushwhackers everywhere in refusing to pay my fare.

CHAPTER EIGHT

A fortune in the sugar country

SUDDENLY, the four of us from the Old Country decided we would leave the bush for ever and go to "the sugar". We decided simultaneously, with no more than a single sentence spoken by the burly Hugh.

We were sitting in the little room at the back of the bar at the "Railway" at Roma, out of the sun on a hot Sunday afternoon. Later, after sundown, the room would be used by the dice school. A two-up game was in progress on the street corner. Hugh and Ted were in for the weekend from their interminable bore-sinking. Hart had lost the sum allowed by his system in the two-up game.

I was out of work, back on the piano banging, filling in vacant hours down by a creek learning the mysteries of Carlo's accordion. (I had vague day-dreams of becoming so proficient that people would pay money for the pleasure of hearing me crashing out sweet old melodies).

A sparsely built little man stumbled into the shade of the empty bar and Gert drew him a pint and herself a snifter of Dutch gin. He looked around for company, and leaning in the doorway of the back room told us he was a boundary rider with nine months' pay, on his way to the coast, and just now he was paying his respects to the town.

That is to say, he was staying at another pub and was now calling at each of the other twelve pubs in the town. This was the custom among visitors. Whether he ever completed the round, or ever got to the coast, I never knew. He was almost sober, and very anxious to talk.

"Bound'ry rid'n," he said, "you don't see a man maybe fer coupla munce. Ration cart brings me tobacco, me flour, tea and sugar, few taters sometimes and a bit of bacon at

Christmas. I'll be out down the fences thirty-forty mile away when the ration cart comes, so I don't see no one. Makes a man talk to his dog, talk to his sheep, talk to the bloody prickly pear.

"Gor stone me, sometimes I think I've done me block. Ev'ry evenin' I'll stand be the door rail of me hut and talk to the crows settin' on the fence. They know I'm tellin' 'em they're every sort of a bastard outer hell the way they takes the eyes outer lambs. Long as I ain't gotter gun they set and stare me out. Sometimes I find I'm talkin' to meself. Youse blokes from the Old Country? Don't never do bound'ry ridin'. Now my brother, he's up in the sugar, doin' fine. Had a letter from him two years ago . . ."

"Whereabouts in the sugar?" asked Hugh.

"Mackay district."

"What does he do, exactly?"

The boundary rider turned his bleary eyes on his questioner. "You never bin up til the sugar, chum?"

"No, not yet. What does your brother do?"

"Do? Grow sugar, chum. He gets a good strong horse, and a plough, and he knocks up a shed, for him and the horse. Then he goes to the mill and the mill gives him twenty-five acres."

"What, for nothing?"

"Not for nothin'. Youse blokes . . . look, they give him twenty-five acres of new land, but it's still their land. Then he goes to the bank and they say they'll stake him for his tucker and tools and seed cane."

"Why do they do that?"

"Why what? Christ." The boundary rider lurched away, but Ted took his arm and sat him down. "Tell us about your brother," he said. "My pal won't ask no more bleedin' questions," he added, glaring at Hugh from beneath his dark brows.

Hart was cleverer. He produced a pint of beer for the boundary rider.

"First year," he said, "me brother ploughs the twenty-five acres and plants the seed cane. Y'know, you plant three notches. Up comes the cane. He sells the cane to the mill

57

and the mill charge him one-and-six a ton for his rent. No crop, no rent. Next year, he ploughs another twenty-five. Then next year . . ."

"But what happens to the first twenty-five?" Hugh, the farmer's son, had to know such things.

The boundary rider turned to him wearily. He was almost asleep. "Don't you know nothin'? Cane grows seven years. First year, not much. Then good heavy cane with plenty of sugar. After five years it ain't much and some folk replant then. Me, I was in the sugar once. Goin' back fer the cuttin' next season maybe." He fell back in his chair, asleep.

Hugh jumped up. "What say we try the sugar?" He spoke the thoughts of us all.

"One week's time," said Hart. "Got to give notice and do the thing properly."

I shared a room at the "Railway" with Ted, the Cockney tram electrician. He was terribly angry, horribly rude about my misfortunes at Charleville, whereas Hugh regarded it as a joke and Hart merely remarked that the police in the Australian bush were now far too highly organised for it to be possible to steal four hundred horses, even if the owner didn't know he had them. Ted scowled and waited until we were alone before blasting and lashing me.

"What about yer ma and pa?" he said. "Fine son you turned out to be—plugged in gaol for bashin' the station-master oughter teach you a lesson. If you'd touched them wayleaves you know what you'd have got? Five years. Five years! Fancy writin' 'ome to your ma you was in prison for the next five years! Coulda bin ten if you'd got them 'orses Of all the bleedin' stupid kids. I reckon you thought you was an 'ero. Blimey, what an 'ero!"

Abashed by his ferocity I said lamely that I trusted Dutch and the others and believed it was all honest and lawful. His comment was that he would be glad to be able to take a stock whip to all three thieving bastards. Not that he could have wielded a stock whip.

After this interlude, I felt his eyes were following me at every step. He never uttered a word in sympathy, but he did say "You better have some money till you get work", and handed me a pound.

But during a walk we took after leaving the boundary rider he became less acrid. The angry light in his eyes died down and his saturnine features twisted into a countenance almost likeable. We were both enthused by the talk of the sugar country and our unanimous decision to go. As described by the boundary rider, the place seemed to offer the sort of chance to carve out the future for which each, in his own way, had looked since we landed.

The idea of the horse and the plough, the iron roof lean-to, doing one's cooking in the evening over the galley fire, adding year by year to the estate—I was already seeing myself hiring men to get on quicker—building a fine house with broad verandahs, having the old folk out, all in a few years! Up in the Proserpine, where they said oranges and pawpaws and bananas grew in the hedges.

I didn't give voice to these secret thoughts. All I said was: "It's what we want, Ted."

His face lit with cheerfulness. "It sounds like it" was as far as he went. "There's plenty of hard work in the bush, Bluey, but nuthin' at the end of it. Least, not so far as I can see. Lousy life, too, fer a man born and bred in the finest city in the world. The ganger out at the bore offered ter teach me enough about runnin' the engine to pass as a third class engineer, but it don't seem to get a man much further."

"You think what the boundary rider said was true, Ted?"

"Sounded true. How can you tell? About here they give you a hundred and sixty acres of pear and ten pound an acre to clear it. We know about that one. It jest breaks fellers' hearts. What bank 'ud lend a man money without security? Banks is 'ard as nails, Bluey. They don't take no bleedin' chances. Still," he said, with a brighter tone, as though he had caught himself in a pessimistic mood, "we're goin' to the sugar, my little pal."

I was exhilarated beyond measure. Back home it was an adventure to go three miles on a tram and stay with Uncle George in the big dark house at King's Cross. Here, in this broad, free country, we decided in five minutes to make a journey of several hundred miles, to new country beyond the Capricorn line, without jobs and with little money. If it was a failure, we might move on another thousand miles.

CHAPTER NINE
Go Norther, they say

AT LAST, here in the coastal rain belt of Queensland, was something like the exotic land built up in our minds back home. It was green. It was rich. Here were great banks of mahogany. Here were furrowed fields of red-brown earth, moist and alive, eager for the seed; endless seas of tall sugar-cane, acres of pineapples growing like cabbages, wine grapes, bananas, corn; orchards of peaches, oranges, fruits I had never seen before. There were hedgerows, and rivers, white-painted houses, real houses, spacious and verandahed.

"Exciting," said Hugh repeatedly. "What a country to farm! Anything would grow here. Any fool could grow it. Just drop in the seed and up she comes."

"The horses look strong and well-fed," was Hart's comment.

Ted stared, fascinated, through the train window. I heard him utter: "Wonder if the pay's any better. Wonder if there's any work?"

"Reminds me of Herefordshire on a hot summer's day after a good night's rain," said Hart. "Powerful loam. Same earth but even better, richer."

There were small birds, too, some gay of colour, some like the London sparrow. Small birds, twittering around human dwellings, completed the sum of this land of fertility and prosperity. It completed a scene which contrasted so sharply with the scene of the blue outback, a dozen crows glaring balefully from a dead tree branch, and a lone hawk gliding above, where no living thing had any special relationship with humans except horses, sheep and flies, and where only the patient Chinese could make a cabbage grow.

"They say it rains here regularly," said Hugh. "Give me twenty-five acres of this land and I'll make a living."

We made for Bundaberg, bypassing other towns as being too near Brisbane to be likely to produce a job. As in all

Australian towns except the capitals, there was no labour bureau, no person or authority responsible for linking the employer with the men looking for work. We knew enough by now, however, to go straight to the police-house. The sergeant looked us over critically, and his eyes came to rest on Ted's tin trunk.

"Settling here," he said. Ted's dark face turned darker, but he said nothing.

"Town's full of blokes wanting work. You might try Fairymead. They're planting."

"Thanks," I said. "Where's Fairymead? Is it a farm?"

"Mill. Few miles out. Nice walk. Youse blokes new in the sugar country? You'd do better further north. Too near Brisb'n here in Bundy. Further north you go, the more jobs and better pay. Still, you could try Fairymead. Big mill, always something going."

In the afternoon we decided to take the walk to Fairymead. There was something familiar, ominously familiar, about the advice that things were better further north. But at the moment we were all like schoolboys going to their first camp, keyed up and excited to see the whole layout of the sugar. The one obstacle to our enjoyment of the walk was Ted's trunk.

All Ted's possessions were in a brown tin trunk, and so far no amount of argument or abuse had persuaded him to get rid of it. It had a padlock and two narrow metal handles, one each side, so that it had to be carried by two people. For some inscrutable reason it was generally agreed by the party that the job of helping Ted carry his tin trunk should fall to me, and there were many moments when I hoped that whoever designed that trunk should have to help carry one for the term of the hereafter.

Having wrapped a rag around the handle I could at first manage a couple of hundred yards. Gradually I improved on this personal record. I cursed freely when the sharp corner swayed into my shin, and often I joined angrily in a free-for-all discussion about the uselessness of tin trunks. Ted always said stubbornly that he preferred the trunk to a leather bag or a swag and if necessary he would carry the thing himself. Knowing this was impossible I never took him up on it. The trunk meant something very special to Ted; something like a hermit crab and the home on its back.

It was a hot day. Every day in these parts was a hot day. But the lane to Fairymead was delightful after the barren bush tracks, and soon on both sides of the lane the land was under crops. We saw cane, some of it giant purple elephant cane, and some no thicker than one's thumb.

The mill came in sight—a great squared-off building entirely clothed in unpainted galvanised iron sheeting. It faced onto a small paddock, at the opposite side of which were the quarters of the hands.

We asked for the boss. "Four of yez?" He scratched his chin reflectively. He looked at my swag and he looked at Ted's tin trunk. He stood thinking. Then abruptly he said "No jobs" and turned on his heel.

But Hart wasn't so easily beaten. "One moment, please," he said, and the ganger stopped and turned.

"I said no work," said the ganger, "but I'll fix for yez to have a feed."

"Thanks," said Hart. "I'm interested in that horse, over there by the tank."

"What about the horse?"

"He's licking some black, treacly stuff from the tap. What is it?"

"Molasses. You new in the sugar?"

"In the sugar, yes, and that's something new to me— horse eating molasses."

"You know anything about horses?"

"Yes. I know that roan is a thoroughbred, and I know he's four years old. He'll get a mile but no more."

"Hum." The ganger reflected. Then he said, "Boss might like to talk to you. Youse other coves kin set there under that mango." He strode off, thumbing Hart to follow.

"Clever," conceded Ted reluctantly. "That Hart's clever. Got brains, that Hart."

"Ah, but he does know horses," said Hugh. "My oath he does."

Hart was back within twenty minutes. "We're in," he said

briefly, and led the way to one of the sleeping huts where we dumped our swags and Ted's lousy tin trunk, washed in cool water, and went across to the meals hut for a good feed.

We had a fortnight's work in the planting. Hart's knowledge of racing and racehorses had "come good"—for the first time so far as I was personally concerned—for the boss had recently been bitten by the racing bug and wanted to talk horses with Hart for a few nights.

After the dry heat of the bush this sugar country was sheer delight. Moist red-brown earth, green, deep green foliage everywhere: the cane leaves, banana fronds, green grass, green trees. Clouds in the sky at times; but large shower clouds which opened and dropped rain and then floated away to leave dense blue skies.

The food was good. Vegetables I hadn't tasted, such as sweet potatoes and pumpkin; and fruits of the tropics. Mangoes tumbled sploshily from oak-size trees, and there were wild orange and lime trees, and guavas in the hedges. Hedges, yes; that was something, too. Lanes between hedges.

It was clear that the warning of the Bundaberg police sergeant was right: we should go "norther". So norther we went. The train took up a part of the way, then we walked into Rockhampton, but straight through and on still norther to Mackay. For this was the place the Roma boundary rider had spoken of. Mackay, he had said, was full of work, opening up all the time. A man could get land at Mackay, too. Land of one's own!

Mackay, as represented by George Blake of Blake's Hotel, welcomed us. That is to say, we weren't thrown out. "Go and see Blake," a sugar hand had advised us further south. "Blake's a towney of yours and a straight-up bloke."

George Blake rubbed his freckled hands through the remaining strands of his sandy hair as he weighed up the four of us standing on the hotel verandah. We were limp and hot.

"Well, come in for gawdsake," he said.

The voice I thought not unfriendly, despite reminding one of the rasp of a file.

A thin, haggard woman came through a curtain into the bar: "What, more of 'em?"

"They'll pay," said Blake laconically. "Give May a shout."

We were in. Hooray for that.

May, a bulky, soft-spoken girl of sixteen or so, showed us our rooms on the upper floor of the two-storey iron-roofed pub. I was last, with a room to myself. I sighed audibly at the luxury of an hotel bedroom, as I dumped my blanket-covered swag on the bed.

"Anything else?" May asked shyly.

"What have you got?" I said. It was a fatuous, impulsive remark which I had heard made by a drunken bushwhacker somewhere outback. Crude, rude. May blushed, smiled and hurried off. I felt stupidly exhilarated.

We answered the dinner gong with alacrity and later George Blake invited us to a conference in the parlour back of the bar. He came right to the point, in a Cockney accent straight out of Smithfield Meat Market.

"Noo up 'ere? No work, no dough? Well, I never barred no one from the Ole Country yet. I'll take yer fer the nex' five er six weeks, but no booze on the slate. Termorrer you git out ter the mill and git yerselves fixed fer a job soon as the mill starts. Cuttin' 'll run till Christmas. Ask fer Mr Todd and say you're from George Blake."

Mackay thrilled us with its flower-bedecked neatness, its tidy sunny streets, fresh-painted houses, its palms, its pretty, smiling girls so smartly dressed. There were soda-fountain bars, and open stores with mountains of juicy fruits.

Beds of flowering shrubs bid us welcome from the centres of the streets. Bougainvillea climbed in masses of purple blossom over the porches and the wide verandahs, and in a park were poinciana trees with their broad mantles of dark crimson flowers. Offshore one could see nearby coral islands of the Great Barrier Reef, breaking the horizon like porpoise humps, idyllic and mostly uninhabited, where one might fish and laze one's life away.

There were many young people here in Mackay, boys and girls in clean white clothes. The place shone with happiness, so that the blue-grey outback country faded yet further from the conscious memory. This Mackay was exciting and, to me, like stumbling into a fairyland. We all felt that we had at last found what we had sought—the Australia of beauty, lush living, and prosperity.

The lane to the big mill was flanked with little trees with ripe guava fruit and sweet lemons, tropical flowers, an occasional pawpaw standing head and shoulders palmlike above the hedgerow. Beyond the hedges were the forests of sugarcane. The smell of the lane was powerful and sweetish, reminding me vaguely of a sweets factory I used to pass as a boy and of toffee-making by my mother.

The mention of George Blake carried a touch of magic. We were all told to report as soon as the cutting started. Mr Todd showed us the sleeping quarters—the wire bunklike beds, one blanket to a bed—and sent us to the cookhouse for a meal. There was milk in the tea and butter in large mounds on the table. After bush grub, this was indeed the Ritz, Ted said.

"Is there any work around here while we're waiting?" asked Hart.

Mr Todd reflected. "You'll get little from the sugar cockies. They don't hire much labour, and jess now they lay off and watch their crops grow heavy. Plantin' the new ground is done. Tell you what, youse can all come out a week early and scrub out the huts."

Passing the next three or four weeks in the little city of Mackay was easy enough. All life here seemed easy— excepting the lives of the Chinese who worked patiently, silently and unceasingly in the two spheres they controlled, the handling of the fruit export, and the inhabitants' laundry.

In the less hot but still warm evenings I had the problem of May. In a year and a half in Australia I had survived the initial battering and had begun to mature physically. My slender frame now carried an extra twenty pounds of bone and muscle. No longer did they call me a tall and skinny Pom. They now said I was long and stringy, and this was almost a compliment coming from men who gloried in their toughness. I had the sun in my bones, and much good meat and toil had gone to the upbuilding of my frame. But until now I had scarcely seen a girl, and about women I knew next to nothing.

For what happened, or didn't happen, with May, I was ready to take all responsibility. May had no brains, but her instinct no doubt told her I would stand by her like a knight of the holy grail if the worst should happen. I had neither instinct nor common gumption. I floundered deeper and deeper, as we sat at nights in the seat not quite wide enough for two under the great mango tree in the yard of Blake's Hotel.

She lay across me, with her eyes closed. She usually wore the thinnest of cotton frocks so that touching her was like touching her nakedness except that the barrier of the frock made the contact more suggestive, nicer too, than contact with her too-warm, damp flesh. I knew, of course, what I was supposed to do, and what I ought to propose, and in fact it was impossible and would have been an insult to have declined to follow the routine line of action between a youth and a girl when the girl signifies.

Moreover, lest it be thought that I was unnaturally moral, or immature, I must add that I was normal if inexperienced; excited and very willing to take my chance with her. At midnight would come the strident call of Mrs Blake telling May to get herself to bed, and one night I said I would come with her. But her room was tiny, and next to the Blakes'.

A swift finishing stroke to the affair was executed, quite accidentally, by Mac the cobbler. Mac was my friend. He was young and just a little chap. (Strange that in this country of brawny six-footers there were many little fellows. Small, tough and fearless, like jockeys.) Mac did the shoe-mending for Mackay, and a good business it was. He was also, like most Australians I met, a fervent gambler.

We four Englishmen, or some of us, would walk into his bright little shop and at once he would close the door, get out the dice, and start a game of hazards on the floor. He used to breathe on the dice, whisper to them, pray to them. But they turned up sevens against him just the same. If we had no money he would get the game going by lending us some, and that as every gambler knows is invariably fatal to the lender.

Still, Hart was heavily in debt by the time we were due to start at the mill. He had invented a special system, and hazards is a game in which a system of chasing good money after bad can be disastrous. Mac was generous, gay and lighthearted. I was happy with him. Even Ted admitted he was a pretty good bloke. Hugh didn't gamble at all. It had no allure for him, especially in a place where good-looking girls abounded.

I was alone with Mac one morning and winning well. I was throwing the main and he was chasing his losses with doubled-up stakes when he happened to say: "You've got May up at Blake's now."

I threw the six, raked the stakes in and cocked the dice again. "You know May?" I said.

"How much are you staking? The lot! Fine, I'll cover it." He counted out the silver. "May? We all know May," he said with a chuckle.

I shook the dice in the leather pot. "You do? How, Mac?" I began to throw.

"Why," he said, as he watched the throw, "she's a push-over. Y'know, if a feller wants a girl he'll wait for May going home of an evening and shove her onto her back. She's easy."

The pot fell from my hand and the dice clattered out. "Mac!" I heard the horror in my own voice. "That's rape, Mac!" He laughed uproariously—not at me, but at the joke of it. "Rape! She likes it, Bluey!"

As I stared, still uncomprehending, he pointed to the dice. "You've thrown your four, Bluey, you lucky long bastard."

I looked at the dice, a three and a one. "It wasn't a throw, Mac. I dropped the pot."

A shadow crossed the glass door. "Quick," said Mac. Before the door was opened the dice had been whipped away and Mac was behind his little counter with a shoe in his hand.

67

"Good morning, Mrs Kortright," he was saying politely. "I have mended your shoes but I want to show you the heels." And so forth. I left quietly and went for a long walk.

Several aspects of the affair came to my mind. The first was the most obvious: if other chaps could push her over, I could too, and with no regrets, no promises and no responsibilities. The second, that this was nevertheless dangerous. The third, that I knew I couldn't push a girl over. And the fourth that the whole business had become disgusting.

Later I asked myself what did I expect—a virgin to fall at my feet? Someone, doubtless, would marry May and she could have six babies in six years and be a thoroughly respectable mother, putting her husband to bed every Saturday night and never mentioning it on the Sunday morning when she brought him a bottle of cold beer.

I avoided May during the remaining few days, and when the mill closed six months later, and the Blakes were living in their own home during evenings, George Blake said: "Bluey, the wife thinks the grub here at the pub isn't what you need to build you up. She says you're to live with us as long as you're in Mackay. Same charge."

Building me up? I had put on another half stone! Mrs Blake, the thin consumptive-looking woman with the accusative pitch in her voice and never a smile on her drawn face, had decided I needed mothering. This puzzled me until one night George Blake, after a third whisky, told me they had had a son who was drowned. "He'd a bin your age, Bluey. Mebbe that's why she feels like I do about kids from the Ole Country."

"Hardly a kid now," I protested.

"You!" he jeered. "You'd get lorst in King's Cross Station!"

I started at the bottom in the mill: the snake-house. Cane from the farms arrived by two-horse open wagon or by little trucks on the portable railway. It was raked onto a slatted elevator which carried it up to the crushers in the upper part of the mill. On its way on the elevator, the loose trash fell through the slatting into a concrete pit.

"Here's a broom and here's a switch of fencing wire,"

said the outside ganger. "You know what the switch is for?"

"If it's for killing snakes, yes."

"Good."

I was on nights, twelve hours less two meal breaks. Ted, having worked on the trams in London, got himself a job to do with the running of the boiling plant, and Hart and Hugh were put straight on to the sugar pans, the hottest, hardest and best-paid job inside the mill. I resented my easy job sweeping cane trash with the occasional excitement of swatting some inoffensive little snake and was later promoted to be the oiler of the trucks.

This, at least, was a daytime job, though as boring as the snake-pit. But there were pawpaws ripening along the truck yards, and the mill food was good—plenty of onion in the meat balls, and no cinders in the steaks and chops. We had cheese, and bacon, and sometimes pies, and there was no limit to quantities. The second helping was larger than the first. I was prepared to leave the bush to the bush-whackers forever.

So we paid Blake what we owed and started to save.

One Sunday afternoon we sought out Mr Todd. We told him what the boundary rider at Roma had said about starting cane growing, and that some of the mill hands seemed to doubt it.

The Australian surveyed us, one by one. I had the uncomfortable feeling that he was trying honestly to discover points in our favour and finding it very difficult. Finally he said: "They'll tell y'anything, some bastards."

It took time and patience to get him talking. For instance . . .

"No truth in it at all, Mr Todd? No land? No bank loan? Doesn't anyone make any money out of growing sugar? Well, then, surely . . ."

"Wouldn't say no truth at all," he finally admitted. "Might be possible further north, up be Cairns, f'r instance. Bloody hot that Cairns."

"No land here at all? Seems thousands of acres within a couple of miles of this mill doing nothing but grow scrub."

"Any land around here that'll grow cane's growin' cane, else it's bin bought and soon will be."

"But the mill, Mr Todd? Doesn't the mill own the land and rent it out?"

"The mill's a company. It ain't a charity trust set up to help immigrants. If it helped anyone it'd help Australians, I should hope. Plenty Australians 'd like the chance of start'n with noth'n but their sweat."

Ted's little black eyes were beginning to throw out warning sparks, and Hart stepped in with his suave, soft manner.

"Mr Todd," he said, "what you say is, of course, perfectly right. Perfectly. We'd feel the same in our country. Or what used to be our country." He let that penetrate and proceeded smoothly. "We don't know what is open to us and what isn't. We can all work our stint and that's what the Australian immigration people expect of us. You'll appreciate that, Mr Todd."

"Too right," said Mr Todd, mollified at once. "Now let me tell youse boys somethin'. You bin in the sugar a few months. You think all you gotter do is git twenty-five acres of beautiful soil, drop in the seed cane and sit on yer arses grillin' steaks while the cane grows an' swells, then you double the patch and jess keep on doublin' up." He swept us with his eyes. "Any one of you ever been on a farm anywhere?"

"I'm a farmer's son—lived my life in farming," said Hugh.

"Good-oh. Then when you git back to tea you can tell yer cobbers that *nothing* grows *anywhere* like that, except weeds and snakes. Farmin's a science and a gamble. Yair, a gamble! You kin be a good farmer and go broke, here like in the Old Dart."

He was warming up now. He banged his pipe on the verandah rail and produced a cake of Yankee Doodle. We watched his experienced fingers cutting thin slivers of plug.

"There was a bloke," he continued, staring at the tobacco he was teasing into a soft ball of loosened strands, "son of a cane cocky up to the Proserpine. Good country, that Proserpine. Same as around here. He got himself a piece of land from this very mill and worked eight years, every day of the year, and especially Christmas Day. The piece was beginning to come good. Ninth year come a typhoon or somethin' and laid the crop flat and useless. Tenth year came the cane beetle and ate the lot. He went broke. Know who that was?"

We all guessed.

"Me."

Noises of sympathy and shock. Sympathy, sincere. Shock, artificial, such is youth's inspired feeling of superiority over failures of the past.

"There's a lot to know about cane. You ever read a book about growin' cane?" he demanded, eyeing each of us in turn. "Well, you kin start there. Then you kin work fer next to nothin' off season for some cane cocky, and find out what he makes. Some gits a tidy living. I'll say that. Stick around in the cane and work and watch, and read, too. Or go north, where they grow heavier cane and bigger beetle. My oath you kin do well outer the cane if the dice fall right and all you ever want out of life is work."

"I reckon," pondered Hugh, after a brief silence, "there's probably as much to know about cane as there is about corn."

"I reckon," agreed Mr Todd.

"Do you happen to have a book on cane?" asked Hugh.

This seemed to shake him. "Matter of fact I do. I'll look it out later on."

And that was that.

"Go west, go north, keep chasing bleedin' rainbows," growled Ted over the steak and tea.

"Trouble with you," remarked Hart drily, "is you came out to Australia expecting to find a nugget of gold under every rock."

"Only one nugget. Jus' one, so I'm sure there's something to work for." Ted's voice suddenly rose to anger pitch. "Something more than lookin' for another bleeding job no better than the one you left."

"Then you'll have to dig for it, as Todd says. Time we all realised that," said Hart. "From what I hear, every small farmer in Australia works seven days a week and so do his wife and family. But he works for himself and one day his farm will come good, as they say out here. Anyway, Todd isn't the last word. He was unlucky, and he's an embittered loser."

"I didn't know about the beetle," I said. "Must be a terrible scourge. You can't go around swatting millions of beetles."

"All these plagues can be beaten," declared Hugh, who had been to a horticultural college. "Mark my words, as soon as these cane people have some research experts on the job to tell them what to do about it, they'll settle the beetle problem. The new theory is, you no longer try to wipe out the pest after it has laid its eggs: you find something that lives on the pest itself, to do the work for you and enjoy the job."

(Prophetic words. One answer to the beetle was absurdly simple—the toad. It ate the beetle and started on the snakes.)

That attractive-looking cane-grower's house we had so often admired, passing along the lane to town, became less sublime as we came closer on a Sunday afternoon. Dad had a wheel off a cane wagon, Ma was driving a couple of cows into the littered yard for milking and son Joey worked stripped to the moleskins and boots on the kitchen plot. The place stank of dung and work, and we saw no sign of anything else.

Hart, Ted and I made for Dad. (Hugh was pursuing a girl.) The farmer looked up and went on with his job.

"Jes' passing," said Ted. "Thought we'd say hullo."

The farmer was clearly astonished at first. "You from the Old Dart?"

"Yes."

"Hum." Which meant, that explains it.

He rolled the wheel towards the wagon. Hart jumped in and helped him work it onto the hub. The farmer wiped his face and sat on a stump, nonplussed to hell.

"If youse boys 've come about the cuttin', it's all set way back. The New Zealand gang always cuts fer me."

72

There was a New Zealand gang, he told us, and a Melbourne gang, and a Sydney gang and lesser fry, and they cut on contracts made separately with each farmer. They cut all through daylight, loaded the wagons after supper, worked six and a half days a week, sometimes seven if there was rain about, and took big cheques down south in time for the New Year.

"They can cut, those boys," said the cocky admiringly. "Christ those boys can cut. Heaviest work I ever saw, and they slash right through the season, farm after farm, keepin' the mill at top stretch till it's worked out. Worth their cheques, them fellers."

"You have had a good crop this season."

The farmer frowned gloomily. "No weight to it. Needed a good rain and another three weeks. But the boys have to start the cuttin' on time."

"But it's a good thing, this cane-growing?" I asked naively. "I mean, the land's fine and a farm like this can be very properous?"

"Prosperous?" He chewed over the thought. "I spose you might say so. Never had time to think about it." Ma was passing. "Ma! Feller wants to know if the farm is prosperous!" It seemed some sort of joke.

Ma glared. "If you come about the taxes the answer's no. If you want a job, it's still no."

This, and the talk with Todd, was not in line with the idea of the sugar country built up in our minds by the Roma boundary rider. Like all previous thoughts on Australia, when one came down to cases the basic truths of opportunity still stood, but the way of achievement reminded me more and more of *The Pilgrim's Progress*. This was no place for dreams and romancing. Even those who had made big fortunes in days gone by had sweated blood and lived dangerous lives.

CHAPTER TEN

But we go west

BUT WHATEVER might lie in the future for us, the present always demanded action. One had to work to keep alive. So, we all worked at the mill. I greased the trucks, Ted did things with the machinery as engineer's mate, and Jack and Hugh shovelled the boiling sugar around their revolving pans until it crystallised. We learned a great deal about sugar and our general conclusion was that the outlook for a farming project, which we had come to seek, was virtually non-existent, but might well be possible either with a little capital, or with luck, or "up be Cairns".

Early in the New Year the cut finished and the hum of the mill died away. The last little trucks came home, and brought the portable rails with them. The elevator rattled no more on its endless belt, and there was no more molten sugar to be hardened and pushed down the pan sinks. Only Ted was told he could go back to the mill after he'd had a spell.

So we came back along the lane into Mackay, turned up the flowered avenue in the centre of the little city, branched to the right near the waterfront, and thence to Blake's. And so to baths, new shoes and strides and white shirts, and a game of hazards at Mac's. So to a good feed or two at Blake's, to some beers (and to me a private feed of rather soft, mildewy chocolates, a much anticipated but disappointing luxury which I thereupon forswore forever in Australia), by which time Hart and Hugh were bored and Ted thought he'd better get back to the mill before someone else snatched his job, with the long workless spell looming up. Hart and Hugh packed their things in bright new suitcases and left for higher jinks than Mackay could offer. They went down to Rockhampton, which had everything a young man with money in his pocket could reasonably ask for.

Then it was that I found myself transferred, like it or not, to the private bungalow of the Blakes, to be given my own corner of the verandah as a sleeping room and the privilege of eating with the Blakes on another part of the verandah. But George Blake and his wife did more: they guaranteed the rent I paid them by getting me a job in the ice factory.

Here, in the little two-man business in a backyard, I worked from four in the morning till noon six days a week, doing the statutory forty-eight hours a week. With little time to spare after a daily session at Mac's, I avoided any further entanglement with May. Possibly, I reflected, this was the initial reason for Mrs Blake's interest in my welfare. I suspected it, but it was never referred to, and there were times when I was tempted to assert my near manhood's independent state by deliberately taking May home.

What stopped me was primarily that May's conversational development had ceased soon after birth, and further the ghastly thought that I should be obliged, morally obliged as it were, to push her over sooner or later. Chivalry demanded it. How did one push a girl, a strong girl, onto her back without hurting her? And how could one equably regard this as a prelude to the sweet, soft murmurings of love-making?

Getting up at three was no hardship. In fact it was a pleasure to do so much of one's shift in the cool. I had an interesting walk to the ice factory at about the hour when the hordes of stinking fruit bats were leaving the inland orchards they had been stripping, to fly back to the mangrove swamps and offshore islands where they hung upside-down all day with folded wings, like rows of smoking kippers at Yarmouth.

I was always first to arrive at the factory and my first job was to stoke up the engine and shovel in some charcoal. Later on came Herman, a tall, cadaverous type, the only person allowed to start the flywheel. This set in motion the freezing plant by pumping ammonia through tanks of brine in which were immersed long squarish cans of water.

Around six o'clock Herman and I cooked our breakfast

and made our tea by the boiler fire, and at eight o'clock we hauled out the cans, knocked out the great slabs of ice and sawed them up into six-inch cubes and put the cubes into the refrigerating house. At nine Herman put the horse into the shafts of the ice cart, we dumped in the ice cubes and covered them with the wet sacks, and off went Herman round the town.

Everyone in Mackay had to have ice. The humblest citizen had to have her threepenny block and the stores and pubs and ice cream bars took dozens. I was never permitted to drive the ice cart, nor to know who bought what. As far as possible, all details of the business were hidden from me. I never saw the boss, but had my wages from Herman. Even the oiling of the donkey engine was veiled in secrecy, and I suspected that the owner of the factory was on a very good thing in flogging the ice and had no wish to invite any interest in his business.

I had written home poetic words in praise of this beautiful and fruitful place and of the prospects of finding at last that dream farm to which my little Welsh Dad and my London-born Mum could retire and help pick the nectarines for breakfast when they felt the need of exercise. But that was on my arrival in Mackay. It was not so easy now to write that I was cutting up slabs of ice for a living.

Dad was getting uneasy. His letters made this very clear to me. He felt I was wandering about too much and gathering too little moss, and was beginning to feel that maybe I ought to go home and find a steady job in an office. He told me the latest news of the Methodist Church, and who was now in the choir, and how the superintendent of the Sunday school, a heavy Scot with a bald head surmounted by a conical bump, had astonished everyone by suddenly moving away with his family from the locality. There was news of the Germans who had opened the delicatessen, selling queer-looking sausage and other foodstuffs regarded with a heaven-knows-what-they're-made-of horror by my parents.

He hoped the church I was attending was Methodist, or if there was no Methodist then Congregational or Wesleyan, but not Wesleyan if avoidable, and he would like to write to the minister. (If I had dared, I would have asked him to write a nice letter to the police-sergeant at Charleville, who had done his best, with his wife, to save me from my best worst friends.)

So the six months' slack passed pleasantly enough, though with no moss accumulating. I gambled with Mac, had Ted for company at weekends for jaunts in the country and around the beaches, and sometimes Mac took us along with his "pack" of young men and girls for a picnic.

Ted and I got along well enough with Mac's friends. They were cautiously polite, but never took us in one hundred per cent. The margin of reserve was always perceptible and one had the feeling they were suspicious whenever we made any reference to Australia or Australians. At any hint of criticism they would jump at us. Why had we come out then? Why not go home again?

I mentioned this to Ted one evening. "Yes, I've noticed it," he said gloomily. "Out west on the job you was accepted if you could pull yer weight. That's all that mattered out there. But even in the west, once you came into a town the same blokes froze you off. Personally, I think it's because England's centuries ahead of this 'ere place and they know it even if we don't say it. And they're so bleedin' proud of Australia they hate to think there's anywhere better or anyone cleverer."

"I'd hate to be there if you ever said all this in public," I said. "Besides, Australia's a long way ahead of England in some matters."

"What matters?"

"Jobs," I said. "We've got jobs. And we eat well. You look five years younger and far fitter than when we first met coming out."

I asked George Blake one night if he felt he was entirely Australian after the twenty-odd years since he emigrated. "Abserlutely, Bluey—all except for one thing." His Australian wife looked up sharply. "Cricket," he said. "Can't help wanting the English boys to lick the Aussies."

It took a long time, he said, to get integrated completely. "You gotter fight yer battles with 'em to reelly know 'em.

You gotter win their respect. You gotter talk plain like they do, even if they don't like what you say." I was reminded of old Yorksheer with his back to the fire in the bush in New South. They certainly didn't like what he said but they respected him. "Make a joke and take a joke. Pay yer whack, and if you're broke, say so. No disgrace in bein' broke out 'ere. And don't be scared of any son of a bitch, because that's fatal with the Aussies."

I respected George Blake's views, and then mentioned the reason we had all come to the sugar country. He hedged. "Miracles keep happening out 'ere. They'll strike oil, or something, one day and no one will be surprised. The fortune is in the land, around 'ere, and its value goes up nigh on every month. But the price of sugar, Bluey, stays where it is at threepence a pound. We can't export it at a profit, so we can't get no further with sugar.

"But why sugar, Bluey? Any mortal thing grows around 'ere. And why farming? There's plenty other ways of a good livin' without sweating in the muck seven days a week and prayin' for rain seven nights, maybe. Plenty of money up 'ere for anyone with brains who'll get down to it and work. This place grows fast. All Queensland grows fast. Now go to bed and think that over in the morning on yer way to the ice factory."

I thought it over, and by next weekend I had a dozen different schemes of making a fortune, all ready to lay out for Ted's inspection.

"You got imagination, Bluey," he said grudgingly. "But all these things need money. Capital. I 'ates the word. But capital we got to 'ave."

The next cutting season came round early in July, and I went back to the mill owing nothing and having saved nothing. Hart wrote that Hugh and he had teamed up with some Rockhampton boys and they were going to cut cane somewhere north of Mackay. "Might not see you till Christmas, but then we'll all get together in Rocky. Must stick together. You never know when we might need each other. So don't lose touch."

Ted had a better job, on the management side, and when

I asked Mr Todd for a chance to earn money he said: "Dreaming of bein' a cane cocky still, Bluey? Well, I've got just the right job for you. Get you into trainin' fer cane growing. Some nice hard work. And when you feel you're fallin' to bits, remember a cane farm's jest as hard, but it's seven days a week and fourteen hours a bloody day."

He took me to the back of the mill and showed me the mill fires. I saw what looked like a brick wall, with the fire doors let into it about three feet from the ground. The wall stood a few feet below ground level, and facing it, on the level ground, was a narrow gauge railway line, on which were already some twenty-odd trucks, all piled up with huge logs, up to eighteen inches thick and upwards of eight feet in length.

"Them logs," remarked Mr Todd, "has to be unloaded off the trucks and rolled down into the pit. That's your job."

"That's all?"

"That's all. It'll kill you in a week I shouldn't wonder. There'll be five men in the pit, the firemen. Every two hours the fire doors are opened, one by one, and the fires filled up to the fire door level with them logs. Don't git near when the fire doors are opened, because the draught's in reverse—outward, not inward. Open the door and out shoots the flame. Understand?"

This was special work, very heavy, very hot, worse than working the pans despite being outdoors. Four hours on, eight hours off on this job.

I thought I had burst a blood vessel in my first session. The logs were so heavy I could not lift them an inch without straining every fibre, every ounce of muscle, from my neck to my toes. After an hour I was utterly exhausted. Dripping with sweat I looked despairingly at the five firemen, who had been sitting smoking, contemplating my efforts without a word.

"Sorry, mates," I gasped. "Can't do it . . . shall have to tell Mr Todd."

They looked at each other with questioning eyes, and seemed to arrive unanimously at a decision. They stood up.

The leader shifted his pipe to a fresh tooth hold. "Now

you watch us," he said to me. Within an incredibly short space of time there was a tidy stack of logs in front of each fire door, handy and neat. The five men returned to their perches.

"Secret is," said the leader, talking apparently to his mates though really addressing me, "to make the log move itself into place. You can't lift them logs, Bluey. It takes four of us to lift a log. Now take a drink of tea and stretch out fer an hour, and then give it another go."

I watched those brawny men feeding the fires. One pair at the front of the log, one pair at the back, each pair having a short steel bar for the lift. The leader surveyed the log, shouted "Hup!" and hooked open the fire doors. Flames shot out a foot. The leader was ready with his crowbar, and as the front of the log was rested on the fire ledge he shouted "Right" and with a mighty shove sent the great log straight through so that it fell to the floor of the furnace endways on.

The front pair, I noticed, wore mittens to the elbow, to avoid singeing, and when the doors were open I could see the reason for the reverse draught: the crushed cane fibre, released from above, had passed through chaff cutters and was descending into the furnace like flakes of snow.

After each furnace was filled the team took a breather, wiped the sweat out of their eyes and tackled the next, until all eight were fired. The operation took perhaps twenty gruelling minutes of sheer, bullocky heaving in hellish temperature, after which they flopped for the remainder of the two hours. It was the hottest and heaviest work I ever saw.

I HAD A CHANCE to redeem myself later on, when the team were firing the eighth furnace, for one of the loaders had a hand pinched by a crooked log and was sent at once to the mill First Aid. I hopped into his place. They hesitated, but only for a second or so, and with a "Hup!" and a "Right!" I carried my fourth of the burden and shoved the logs into the flames. No one thanked me, and I had enough sense to make no comment. I had long since learnt that lesson—"Do it; don't yabber!"—how long ago? a hundred years?

They were good to me, those brown men with ox-like torsos. I needed help with the log-rolling for some time, my worst being at the start of a shift, when all the accumulated aches and pains and feelings of exhaustion crowded on me. But, as with other jobs, my body throve on the work. I ate double.

Within a month I could turn off those logs and play them just where they should go, rogues included, and sing a song at the same time. I could also take an occasional turn at firing, so that we became a six-man team, sharing work, smoko and meals.

This, I think, was the happiest six-month period of my whole life so far as I had then lived it. I could feel myself growing in strength, and I knew that henceforth there would be few jobs requiring just physical effort which I could not do. I was still long and stringy, and always would be, but my back was straight and well covered with muscle and that, they said, was the key to strength and endurance.

Hugh and Hart came down to Blake's for a weekend with us in mid season. Their contracts had many gaps and some of them were not panning out well, but they seemed to be fairly satisfied. "It's heavy," said Hart, "but not too heavy. There's no fortune in it. Still, we should have a tidy sum when we cut out, around Christmas."

Hugh was excited about a fruit cocky he had been having a series of talks with. "Give me modern equipment, let me use modern methods," he was saying between pints, "and I could get a tremendous yield per acre up there. This chap's willing to take me in as full partner if I can raise the cash. I'm writing home about it. They can have the cane. I'll take the orchards. With forty or fifty inches of rain every year as regular as clockwork, hot sunshine on good brown earth, it's a farmer's paradise. All you need is labour, good fruit packing, and some modern plant and sprays."

"He's got something, I think," commented Hart. "There are big possibilities."

"What sort of cash?" I wanted to know.

"A thousand pounds," said Hugh. My heart sank. My father couldn't have sold his house for a quarter of that sum, even if it hadn't been mortgaged.

A thousand pounds! "Your old man must be rich," I said.

"He's always moaning about the weather and his crop failures, but he doesn't fool me," said Hugh, darkly. "He sent me out here just because I got a girl in the family way. Well, if he wants me to stay out here so that he can stand for parliament without being embarrassed, he'll have to foot the bill."

So now I knew why Hugh had emigrated, and why Ted had come (near starvation) and why I had come (incurable dreaming of adventure and fortune). We had yet to know why Hart had left the paternal nest and what sort of nest. Probably, I thought, we never would know.

Our mill finished in the third week of December. Hugh and Hart were already in Rockhampton and we decided to join them. Ted and I had had eighteen months without a break. We had earned well, and the cautious Ted observed that it would cost very little more in Rockhampton than living in Mackay and mightn't be quite so hot so that one wouldn't need to drink much. Ted had been very, very poor. He was determined never to be so poor again.

Three weeks later I began to realise the change that was gradually taking place in Ted, under the softening influence of the cushioned life on the coast. I was in bed, with a mild attack of some sort of fever. It was very hot in the bedroom we shared, though the double doors were wide open to the upper verandah. It was afternoon, and Ted sat in the doorway in his thin pyjamas. (We all had new pyjamas, new suits, fancy hats and shirts, and patent shoes. Hart had insisted that clothes were always important in a town.)

"It's a problem, what to do next, chum," said Ted, chewing on his cigarette. The way he looked into nothing made him appear more short-sighted than usual. "You and me, we ain't ever goin' to own no cane farm, nor no other bleedin' farm. We ain't farmers. We ain't nothing, Bluey. At least, not yet. But I keep thinkin' what ole Blake said about opportunities, and openings. There's plenty of labour in

82

this country, pal, better'n anything you or me can do. But we come from where people got to use their loaf, else they starve."

I wasn't feeling up to joining in an argument so I listened. Any other time I would have argued even if I'd agreed with him, for Ted was the sort of man who invited an argument, almost forced you to argue with him. This day, I had a new Ted.

"Yus, we've 'ad two seasons in a sugar mill. But, chum, there ain't no future there fer us, not jus' labouring. We'll never own no mill, nor a single stick of cane. You bin earning good money. I bin doing a more responsible job than anything I've done before over here, almost as responsible as the night I had to take a tram singlehanded through the traffic to the terminus at New Cross and never drove a tram before in me life.

"It's made me think. Maybe I never told you before, Bluey, but the last three months I was sort of assistant manager at the mill, checking accounts, sorting out tangles in the transport section, getting the raw sugar out to the wharf. When they found the molasses tanks overflowing they sent for me. I organised, Bluey, and I think I done it well. Bluey, with another couple years I could manage that bleedin' mill myself!"

He was saying it to convince himself it was true. I felt that Ted had been astonished to find he could do what he had done.

I made a feeble attempt at a joke about being sure of a job myself in that event, but Ted brushed it off angrily.

"Can't you see, fathead? Can't you see the wood fer the trees? We've bin tackling Australia the wrong way. They always told us they didn't want to be saddled with more unskilled labour. Well, there ain't no trams in the bush, and you never went to work before you come out. So we joined the queue for unskilled labour. But you got good schooling, Bluey, and I got a bug for management!"

He lit another cigarette, then surprised me by asking: "This upset you, this smoking?" Ted was even becoming polite.

"And I'll tell you something else, chum." He took a long draw, watched the exhaled smoke curl upward, and then dropped it quietly: "I'm not going back to the mill."

That shook expostulation from me from a dozen angles. He listened patiently and then said, without a trace of his old sarcasm: "Bluey, boy, that Mackay's a damn nice place, and Mac's a damn nice hazards player, and it's all damn nice living around there. But where will you finish? Still labouring, and like as not in a few years married and having kids and loitering around the pubs till the mill starts again.

"Now lie back, old pal, and don't get all excited and indignant. You can't see yourself as you'll be in five years, but I can, if you peg down in Mackay. Of course you'd marry and have kids. You're 'uman, ain't you? You wanter sleep with a woman, don't you? Well, it's bound to happen, but you didn't oughter let it happen till you've found what you're lookin' for. Now Bluey, you tell me where the future lies for you in the sugar?"

I was trembling slightly with fever and my voice was high pitched as I shouted at him, "You tell me where else it is! Where? Where? Where?"

I knew it was true but I hated him for making me realise it. Life in Mackay had been fine, even luxurious and Ted was snatching away the golden curtain that had hidden from view the emptiness of the future.

"I know," he muttered. "That's what I said, chum. It's a problem. It's a problem what to do next. We got to find the answer, got to go on searching. It's here, somewhere in Australia. I can sorter feel it's here."

If I was growing up physically, Ted was growing in wisdom. Ted was using his loaf.

Nevertheless, the problem of what to do next solved itself two weeks later and in a manner not in the least surprising when you think about it. Jack Hart was in trouble. Jack Hart had been to the races again.

Only once before had I seen Hart display any sense of urgency, and that was when he slugged a man in that Brisbane pub late one night and fought to get me out of the ensuing melee. Usually, he had an ice-cold control of whatever he said and did. But on this occasion his narrow, sensitive fingers beat a nervous little tattoo on the bar table.

"Boys," he said, "I've got to get out of Rockhampton. Now! Tonight!"

"Horses," guessed Ted.

Hart nodded—just a gesture of confirmation and not of regret. After a short silence he seemed to gather control in order to make a statement. Very rare for Hart, whose code of living did not include explanations of his personal affairs.

"Everything went wrong today. Couldn't have been worse. Five favourites on the trot went down the hill. I reckoned I must get out if I doubled up, and I finished losing every cent. I had been winning regularly and the system was doing fine. Consequently I'd been running up bills all over the town. I really believed I'd found a system that couldn't lose. As a matter of fact it only loses now through lack of capital. I've been spending money as I did when . . . when I had plenty of it, in the old days. Now I'm in a mess—temporarily, of course."

"Perhaps we can help," Hugh suggested, not convincingly. But Hart declined immediately.

"Too much," he said. "I might perhaps accept a loan of a few pounds to settle with this hotel. Otherwise the bill will be in your laps when I've hopped out."

"Hopped out where?"

Ah! that was the question that interested us all.

"There's only one place," said Hart at once. "The sugar country's dead for months and there's nothing else here on the coast except the meat factory, and slaughtering isn't my idea of quiet fun. But there's the west. There's always the west."

"The one place," said Hugh, "where I don't wish to go. Nothing but flies, sand, sweat, no work and no hope."

"How d'you know that?" Ted shot at him. "You never bin wester than Roma."

"Just a minute." Hart smoothly took over. "I got myself into this mess. All the people I owe money will be paid, in time, but you chaps don't owe me any loyalty over this.

Let's see this quite clearly. You don't have to come with me."

He looked in turn at each of us. For the life of me I couldn't visualise Hart, who always faced everything that came, turning his back on trouble and sneaking out of town, It was unreal, but clear that he would when it suited him.

Ted's thoughts were in a different track. "In a matter of a few weeks," he said, "if we stay here in Rockhampton, we'll all be broke. Then what? I'm not waiting here, nor in Mackay, running up debts waiting for the next cane-cutting season to start, and with just the same story at the end of it. I'm going west myself, anyway. It makes sense ter me. What about you, Bluey? Let's 'ave your views. You've seen some of the outback. We 'aven't."

Hart nodded. "Good point, Ted. But hurry. I'm packing shortly."

Much flattered, I said: "If we go west we must hump the bluey. How far? I don't know. But we must hump it until we find work, and you can't find work riding in a train. We must find work and then get around and have a look at the west." I paused.

"We may have to hump it hundreds of miles, and in that case we'd be mad not to stick together. But don't think I know the west. It seems to me it's a different country which-ever part of it you find. Sometimes no water. Sometimes no work. But I feel pretty sure we won't starve. Not now. We can get by until we've really seen the west."

Hugh had been thinking. I could read his thoughts with ease—no reply expected from his old man for three or four months, reckoning six weeks each way as the minimum time for letters. That thousand pounds wouldn't be in the envelope, either. The battle would not be won so easily . . .

"Might as well come," he said, and smiled gaily, as though a load had suddenly lifted from his mind. "Things are getting involved here," he explained, "and one ought to see the west, though I can't see this swaghumping exactly like the Lord Mayor's Show."

Hart, having listened to each of us, and studied each face, then said: "It'll have to be tonight."

In our bedroom as we packed, Ted and I indulged in some plain speaking. I said: "Ted, that tin trunk of yours goes no further so far as I am concerned."

And he said: "I'll bet my Aunt Fanny's virginity you'll be glad to get out of this town. Why on earth can't you let these tarts alone? This Mollie. Gaw' blimey!"

"It wasn't my fault," I protested, on the defence at once, "wasn't hers either. It just happened. These things do, you know."

He half choked an exclamation of contempt.

"Anyway," I added, "it finished this afternoon. Finally and forever."

Ted asked no questions. He just grinned and said: "Well, bear up, Bluey. Plenty more fish in the sea. Bleedin' good ones, too, I reckon, if you ain't in too much of an 'urry. I'll put the trunk in at the railway station luggage office if you'll give me an 'and."

CHAPTER ELEVEN
My Irish Mollie

MOLLIE. This Mollie, he called her contemptuously. A demure Irish lass with raven hair and blue eyes, roguish eyes, a lilt in her voice and a swing in her walk. Buxom, comely Mollie. Demure, did I say? It depended what was in a man's mind when he looked her over and when she looked at him.

Mollie was my third exploit with the female sex. The first female implored me, demanded of me, that I should leave the ship at Fremantle and marry her forthwith. She was from Enfield and was going to be a domestic servant. She was anaemic and an orphan, several years older than I was, and she said I was the first human that had ever been kind to me. Having practically nothing of earthly value, she offered me the only treasure an orphan girl could offer, and not knowing what she had in her mind, I declined to be interested. I wasn't quite sixteen.

The second adventure was May, who demanded nothing but offered everything. Both these situations I could understand enough to deal with. But Mollie, you couldn't classify her as this or that. She was unpredictable, mysterious, beyond masculine understanding, entirely without any sense of logic. I could probably add, too, impregnable.

She came into my life a week or two before Ted raised the big problem of where-do-we-go-next. I had been aware of her delightful smile, her beauty, her freshness, her trust and sincerity. On the very first day I went to bed with my fever she bustled into the bedroom looking efficient in her white starched apron, put her cool hand on my brow and said to Ted: "This young man's ill. Did ye know that? Ye did so? Now out ye go and let him sleep quietly. Get along wid ye."

She hustled him out, darkened the room and sat beside me, and despite my protest that I wasn't ill at all she took my temperature, cooled my head with cold compresses, gave me medicine for the fever and then sat quietly, holding my hand.

Well, not to make too much of it, I liked it. After all, Mollie was all woman, lovely, ample woman. And when, in the evening, she remade my bed, gave me fresh cool pillows, stroked my head until I was sleepy, and finally gave me a motherly, brushing kiss before stealing quietly away, well, I liked that, too.

My problem was to know whether it was all entirely motherly, and if so how so young and lovely a person could be motherly anyhow. Very confusing. I speculated on her age and reckoned her between twenty-five and thirty, but Ted, who disliked her on sight, put her at ten years more, which was ridiculous.

However, the affair progressed; no mistake about that. As I recovered she kissed me quite a lot, practically on request, as it were. But there was always a degree of restraint in everything. Her kisses were the sort a girl might give to a brother of whom she was very fond, full-blooded but not sexy. I could fool around with her when it was dark, and quite suddenly it was as though she had only just noticed it and was shocked.

Was I in love? Hooked? Not with the barb. She could have hooked me quite easily, and I would have had nothing to be ashamed of, for Mollie was a good looker and well made, as I have said. Any man in Rockhampton would have whooped at a chance of seducing her, and the single men would have married her if necessary.

We went a few walks together, but discreetly. Mollie was jealous of her reputation. Myself, I never dared contemplate the end of it until too late. Mollie was too strong. The end, I always felt, would be as she wanted it.

And then, one afternoon when I was with her in her linen closet, came the cane-cutter from Townsville.

They called him Jack. Everyone knew Jack, a swarthy young giant whose muscles threatened to split his singlet apart. Jack came bounding into the hotel, up the stairs four at a time, shouting "Mollie? Mollie? Hey Mollie!" She walked straight out of my light embrace into the great muscular hug of the cane-cutter. I watched aghast as he caught her up and kissed her and kissed her again.

Mollie enjoyed as much of this as she chose and then broke away, and I saw that Jack was a fine, handsome man, with a gay manner and an easy smile. He looked at Mollie with pleased anticipation. He expected women to fall for him, and no doubt they did. Myself, he never even noticed, though I stood no more than a yard away, and Mollie, too, seemed to have completely forgotten I was there.

"Where's my room, Mollie?" he said urgently. "We're goin' out tonight, Mollie, and to hell with your job in the bar!"

Mollie led him away without so much as a glance at me, and they disappeared into a distant room. I stood awhile, maybe ten minutes, upset and anxious to talk it all out with Mollie. Then she came hurrying back, and smiled her old, intimate smile.

"Mollie!" I called.

"Busy now," she called back, quite pleasantly and casually.

Then the big Townsville cove came back. He ignored me, and went down the stairs three at a time as light as a cat. There was a woman's scream from the kitchen, followed by women's laughter and the strong happy voice of the Townsville man. No place, not even the kitchen, was safe from Jack.

For a couple of days and nights I moped around the place, never able to get Mollie to myself for a moment. I felt angry, mortified, treated like an old toy kicked into a corner. Maybe she was engaged to the Townsville man, and maybe she thought he had run out on her, and now he'd turned up again, the prodigal lover. Well, if it was like that, she ought to have the decency to tell me.

But Mollie flitted about, humming happily, nodding to me and waving me off with a smile and a joke, as though nothing had happened to affect our love affair except that she was busy. Whenever the Townsville cane-cutter wanted his early morning tea, or his shaving water, or his clean shirt, he pounded down the balcony past my room shouting "Mollie! Mollie! Hey, Mollie!"—like a man calling his dog. The possessiveness of it stung me.

After a couple of days I heard voices, angry voices, from Mollie's pantry, and the cane-cutter came out, shouting and cursing, and shuffled heavily down the stairs. He went into the bar, started a fast drinking bout, and an hour later he left the pub.

I found Mollie alone in her little curtained pantry that evening.

"Hallo, Bluey," she said softly.

I found it hard to speak, and she saw I was agitated and upset. "Come into my room," she said, and took me by the arm with soothing fingers.

We sat on her bed, side by side, and I looked around me in wonderment. Dresses, stockings and strange white cotton garments hung over a chair. There was a pink silk nightdress on her pillow. Her dressing table was filled with a collection of bottles and boxes. On one wall was a coloured picture, neatly cut from a brandy advertisement, of a beautiful nude sitting on a rock. The room's odour was concentrated female: scent, clothing, peppermint (I thought possibly schnapps), woman, all a bit stale and suffocating in this hot little room.

I had only once before found myself in a woman's bedroom, and that one, belonging to the young Brisbane tart Sheila, had been a good deal more pleasant than this. I would have got out, if I could, for that room suffocated all ideas of lovemaking, but with Mollie beside me sitting close with her arms around me inviting me to take the next step, I was hopelessly on the spot.

"Now," she whispered, "what will it be troublin' yez? Tell Mollie."

By now I wasn't even sure what it was about, but she held me fast, physically and by her questions, and I had to come out with it.

"That cane-cutter," I said.

I felt her freeze momentarily. "What about him?"

"Well," I said, quite unable to choose my words

cautiously, "he seems to mean a great deal to you, and I thought we—that is, you and I—were going to make a do of things, if you get my meaning."

"Make a do of things?" She drew away and stared at me. I couldn't believe she was bluffing, or didn't know how I felt. Yet it seemed so.

"Mollie," I started again, "you know we've been very, well, friendly. I can't talk like people do in love stories, but I thought it was serious, and now this Jack comes along. You see, Mollie," I said, trying hard now to fence a way out of it, "I really only want to know how things stand between you, but if you don't want to tell me it doesn't matter. I oughtn't to have asked."

She sat back and looked at me for several seconds. It seemed to me she found it difficult to believe something about me and eventually came to understand, for her look softened, and she smiled at me. And this wasn't the customer's smile, nor the flirt's smile.

"You don't have to worry about him, Bluey, dear," she said gently, and putting her other plump arm about my neck she drew me to her and kissed me full on the mouth. It was a long, tender kiss, and its effect on me was devastating. I grabbed her as I had never grabbed a woman before, and kissed her with hard lips until she broke the clinch and flopped back on the bed, bruised, amazed and exhausted. I felt now like any man should. I felt like going on.

"My God," Mollie gasped, "you're pretty rough."

"Mollie, darling," I said, hardly knowing what I was saying in my excitement, "we've got to do something about this. Pretty quick."

She was up off her back in a flash. "Do something? Do what?"

Now I floundered. "Well," I said, "something. Obviously it can't stop like this. Get married or something, for instance."

"Hell," said Mollie, "you're joking, surely?" She looked hard at me. "Us? Married?"

"No," I said, babbling foolishly and knowing it was foolish. "I'm not joking, Mollie, though I realise it wouldn't be very easy going for a while. But you do know we've been about together, in a way courting. Well for my part," I added, "that's fine, especially after the way you just kissed me—well, we want each other, if you know what I mean." So difficult I found it to bring it right down to sex. The code of that old Methodist chapel back in North London still had me pinioned.

Mollie spoke softly again. "I didn't know it went that far. It shouldn't have. Bluey, it all sounds very nice, about getting married, but we must be practical, mustn't we? For instance, where do we live? What on?"

"That's my worry," I said and tried to grab her again. She shoved me away. "I can get a job down at the ice factory at Mackay," I said, "and maybe we can get a bit of land . . ."

"You can't eat land, me darlin' boy."

But I went on yapping about working day and night, about the play I was writing, and various other schemes I had of making a quick fortune, and she seemed glad to listen though I was happily aware I wasn't breaking the ice.

I broke off suddenly. There was a familiar pounding on the uncarpeted stairs and a strong deep voice bellowing: "Mollie! Mollie!"

The door of Mollie's bedroom was flung open and the cane-cutter filled the doorway with his broad frame. "What's this?" he growled.

Mollie stiffened and her jaw shot up. "I told you to come to this room when you were asked," she snapped at him. "Get out."

He appeared not to hear. Looking at her, and pointing to me, he said: "Is this the bloke?"

"What bloke?"

"Is this the bloke that takes you square-pushing of a night when I'm out of town?"

He hitched his trousers, and his muscles gleamed and flexed. Beads of sweat shook off him. I got off the bed. There was little room for evasive action but my mind was working at chaotic speed to get me somewhere safe somehow.

Not so Mollie. "You get out of here," she screamed at him. She pushed me back onto the bed and pulled my arm around her waist. "What I do and who I marry is my affair. You can blow."

I tried to get a word in here, tried to get to my feet again, but Mollie was strong and at this moment she was fierce as an eagle.

"You shut up, too," she said to me. "You've begun enough trouble already."

"What I'm asking is," said the cane-cutter in sullen anger, "are you or are you not going to marry this Pommie bloke?"

"Yes, she is," I said impetuously.

"Because if you are," he said to Mollie, "I'll kill him."

Mollie pulled me back again and jerked my arm around her waist. I must have looked a fool, sitting beside her like that, and now I noticed how hard and unyielding, unfeminine, her corsets were. Oddly, this produced some feeling of security.

Mollie moved her free hand to her dressing table and picked up a pair of long scissors. "If you touch him," she said, her Irish brogue strong now, "I'll hack your eyes out, you dirty bushwhacker. He's worth ten of you. He's a gentleman, not a drunk growing a pot belly loafing around pubs. And why shouldn't I marry him? Who are you in all this?"

The big cane-cutter wilted somewhat. He had known Mollie a long time, and my guess was that he knew she wasn't bluffing. At the moment Mollie looked capable of bundling into a herd of elephants.

"What's the idea?" said the cane-cutter, with a frown. "You can't do this to me after all the years we've known each other."

"Too long," said Mollie. "Two years it's been, and it's done me no good at all."

"You never talked this way before," he said.

"You come here every once in a while," said Mollie, "and you think you've bought the whole damn pub, women and all. Then you beat off somewhere else where there's other girls. You fancy you're a hell of a feller. Now you

94

think you've bought the right with a couple of drinks to tell me when I can't get married."

The cane-cutter was possibly no great brain, but he understood with painful clarity the logic of what she said.

"I never thought about it that way, Mollie. You know I was always pretty fond of you. You was always the one that mattered. Kinda tough, suddenly finding you stuck on some immigrant kid and going to marry him."

I was feeling more comfortable in my mind now, and rather sorry for the big Townsville man. He looked a decent chap. Physically I was not so happy. Mollie's body was hot against mine and her face, flanked by streaks of hair, was creased and forbidding. The air was stifling. I felt like a boy who has stumbled into a grown-ups' wrangle, which I was.

"Well," said Mollie, firmly if somewhat less angrily, "you should've thought of that."

He waited, hitting a fist into a huge palm.

"That is," added Mollie, "if it really is kinda tough. Plenty more women waiting for you, no doubt."

He shook his head dolefully. "I don't want 'em. Matter er fact, Mollie, I jest bin out a few miles on a proposition."

"What sort of proposition?"

"Feller I know. Wanted me fer a partner in cane grow'n'. Good piecer land. Nice house, too. Asked me if I wanted to sorta settle down."

"What did you say?"

"Turned it down. But when he told me he'd heard about you was going around serious with some bloke, I thought . . . y'know . . ."

"You thought what?"

"Why," he said with some difficulty, "I thought maybe it wouldn't of been too bad of an idea if we'd got married, you and me, and set about getting a home and a coupla dawgs, and I'd plant some fruit while the cane was settin', and we could have some kids, maybe. I thought we'd go down to Brisbane for a honeymoon first, and a look at the racin', and then come back and, oh, what the hell."

There was a pause.

"Seem you have been thinking," said Mollie tartly.

"Well," said the cane-cutter, and subsided.

I felt sick. I wished myself a million miles away, even in grubby old North London's yellow brick dormitory. I could neither release my arm from Mollie's large waist, nor move an inch within her fierce clutch, but was forced to sit huddled up to her on the bed and stare at the big feller moping and sweating by the door. The shackles of my love had now completely dissolved into the gin-soaked air. I wanted to get out. Quickly.

"What's in your mind now?" asked Mollie at last.

The cane-cutter flapped his hands. "I've asked you to marry me. Can't expect a bloke to say it all over again."

"I never heard you," she said.

"Well," said the cane-cutter, "I'm asking you now."

It occurred to me, but dimly, that now was the moment when I should speak, make a violent protest as perhaps a man of honour should, or brand myself as a coward for ever, by holding my peace. The fact was, I was too hot to bother.

Quite suddenly I experienced a blessed release. I was tossed aside like a discarded petticoat as Mollie bounced up from the bed, her perspiring face suffused with the glory of a woman who has found her soul mate. She poured her chubby form into the arms of the cane-cutter, and their embrace was an example of human juxtaposition amazing to behold. The cane-cutter at last had what was coming to him.

Amid their happy murmurings I staggered to my feet. Sportingly I extended a hand to the winner. "Congratulations," I said hoarsely. "And the best of luck."

Neither heard me. Now they were kissing and laughing and changing the clinch. I made for the door. It was blocked by the entwined bodies.

"Pardon me," I said. I had to say it twice.

The cane-cutter looked over Mollie's shoulder. "Oh, sure," he said, and shuffled his blissful burden aside.

CHAPTER TWELVE
Moonlight Blondin walk

"ODD THING IS, we do look like the Lord Mayor's Show," said Hugh.

"More like Fred Karno's 'Night Out'," Ted retorted, not unhappily. "Funny in a way that no one seemed to see anything peculiar as we come up through the town. Jack with 'is fancy 'at and fancy suit and clocks in 'is socks and a swag over 'is shoulder, and Bluey rattlin' the cookin' cans, and Hugh with the tucker bags and me with the water bags . . . if we'd walked down the Old Kent Road like this some cop woulda 'ad us in the clink."

We trudged up a hill and in a copse at the top we stopped as one man, dumped our cargo and sat down to wipe the sweat away and enjoy the evening breeze coming up off the Pacific.

Hart spoke for the first time since we left the hotel. "I had reckoned," he said quietly, "on opening a couple of bottles of champagne for us, I was so sure I'd made a killing. However, this is just as good when you're thirsty." He pulled out two quart bottles of English beer. "No sense in carrying them any farther."

Out came the new pannikins. "Success in the west," said Hart. We drank to that.

Hugh was exhilarated by the view. Below were the lights of Rockhampton, with the glare of the meat factory standing out and away, and to our right the river mouth and the sea. "If I never see Rocky again," he said, "that was a bust I'll never forget. Best in my life. Everything right—the girls, the beer—well, for Australian it wasn't bad," he added quickly as he saw protests coming—"I mean, it's the same brown flat stuff that comes out of the barrel anywhere here in Queensland but at least it was less warm.

"There was the kinema—wonderful, these moving pictures, and what a place to take a girl! And the fun on the river, the shops—Rocky's got the lot. It's alive, and full of money and noise and movement. That's where I'm going with my next cheque."

No one disagreed.

"When we go back," added Hugh, "we'll know when to go to the sugar, and how to get the cutting contracts before the Melbourne and New Zealand teams step in and clean it up. Some of those chaps left with over a hundred pounds apiece. That's real money, even if it's hard work."

"Waste of labour," said Ted. "Sheer waste of labour. They can't know nuthink about electricity up 'ere, drivin' that mill with wood fires. Don't be surprised if the mills are all electric when we get back."

"Can't see that," murmured Hugh. "You can't have anything electric or mechanical in agriculture. You need strong, short-back draught horses for our work."

"You can take it from me," said Ted. "and I'm an electrician and I know what I'm talking about. They can run anything on electricity. If they can run a tram they can run a bleedin' plough. Soon they'll be runnin' trains on electricity, you'll see. They'll cut cane by electricity—and load the trucks!"

"Who cares?" This was Hart. "The only people, apart from the mills, who will ever make money in Mackay are the Chinese laundries and the Chinese fruit exporters—oh, and the pubs. Now that Blake, who ran the pub where we stayed, he was a clever immigrant. Blake never worked in the bush, nor in the sugar. He always had someone to cook his dinner. Blake's a smart little Cockney, smarter than you, Ted. You're humping your swag, while he's married to the Australian girl who owns the pub. He soon found how to pull beer and when to give short measure. Well done, Blake, me boy."

I hated Hart in this sarcastic mood. "I don't think Blake was too bad of a bloke," I said. "He helped me. He just had no sense of humour."

"Too bad?" Hart sat up. "Bluey, he was the best feller we've met. Took us in when we were skint, stood us on the slate until we got work. He's been out here sixteen years, and he's Australian in everything except he still drops his aitches. He'll help any lame duck, whether he comes from Sydney or Manchester. He's made himself nice and cosy, with his private villa, and he's steadily packing his profits away . . ."

"They had a fine mango tree in the yard," I said absently.

". . . but Blake's not the type that Australia needs. We are far better value to this country than he is. We work with our hands, and produce, and take a share in developing Australia. But it seems to me more than fifty per cent of men and women from the Old Country either stay in the towns or go back home because they never should have come. Like you, Bluey, in your first year. You must have been near to going home, especially after the Charleville affair, weren't you?"

"Funny thing, no. My only fear," I said, "is of having no friends. I don't find Australians easy to be real friends with. They treat you fairly, but they take a lot of understanding. In fact, the only Australian, so far, that I've made a real friend of was Mac, the little chap with the shoe shop in Mackay.

"Remember how he used to bring out the dice from under the counter whenever we went in? A terrific gambler. But he used to give me my money back when I lost and say: 'Pay me when you get your cheque'. Last time I saw him I owed him three pounds, and he said: 'I'm going down to Brisbane. But you'll pay me sometime. I know that, Bluey.' So I will, too."

"I get on with Australians pretty well," said Hugh. "No trouble at all."

"That," said Ted, "is because you're a big tough bullocky feller."

"Exactly. And they're right," said Hart. "We live with the manual types out here, but don't imagine they're not just as proud of Australia as the prime minister himself. This country needs the tough chaps, the tree fellers, the shearers, the drovers and the boundary riders and the dawn-to-dusk cocky farmers. Every Australian knows it even if he's never thought about it. Hugh's got what the country

99

wants, and if you haven't got it they don't see why the country should keep you alive."

"And Bluey," said Ted, "has got to live by his brains." Which I took to be a dig at Australia on the one hand and a piece of oblique sarcasm in case I should be tempted to feel flattered.

"Time we were off," said Hugh. "Jack, I'm afraid you'll have to wear my beautiful suede town shoes. You certainly won't get far in those patent leather things. Fortunately I've got myself a good stout pair of boots and I'd think these suedes will last you quite a while."

Hart took them without comment.

We moved westward, on a lane alongside the railway track which was to be our guide for hundreds of miles, and split into pairs. Hart manoeuvred to be with me, behind the others, which surprised me.

He talked of this and that in quiet friendly fashion. This happened very rarely, but when it did, Hart was quite irresistible. He had a peculiar charm and his voice carried a quality of deep and sincere interest in whatever I said, no matter how trite. After a bit he said casually: "By the way, I always wondered what happened in the end of your tangle with that big Irish chambermaid?"

He forestalled a possible rebuff by adding at once: "I could see you were getting into serious trouble, and when the big cane-cutter came along I was around in case of need."

"Well, thanks," I said, surprised. "I didn't know you knew anything about it. I mean, it was just between Mollie and myself."

"Bluey," he said, but without sarcasm, "you don't imagine you can go walking with a female along dusky lanes in a small town without the whole town talking?"

"I see," I said, and hitched my swag to a less uncomfortable position. Carrying a swag, a one-shouldered, one-handed job, needed a certain technique which one acquired through soreness and fatigue. "Well, of course Mollie was a bit old for me."

"Old?" said Hart. "I'll lay the odds she's thirty-five,

probably with five or six small children back home waiting for the call when Mama gets married."

The idea left me aghast.

"Well," said Hart, "let's consider it fairly. You'll admit Mollie is still a good looker? Bit heavy for my style, but lots of men like 'em that way. She has a fine healthy complexion, she has what men like, if you know what I mean, and she is the sort of woman that likes men.

"Don't take that as bad form, Bluey, but just a biological observation. She comes from Ireland, where they have large families, and she's only been out here two or three years. It's just not possible she wasn't married at least ten years before she emigrated, and the fact that she's looking for a husband indicates that the first one is now safely out of the way. Personally, Bluey, I think you've been lucky to get away."

I walked in silence, but Hart guessed what was passing through my mind and presently said casually: "Mollie's the type Australia needs, and that cane-cutter's what Mollie needs. They'll have six more kids in ten years, and with Mollie's six coming over from Ireland that's a dozen. What a lot of immigration costs this country will save!"

"I don't believe that rubbish about her having six kids."

"Maybe not. Maybe I'm wrong. But I'll take slight odds she'll have six now, and they'll be strapping, big-boned youngsters, every one of them, all cane-cutters."

I wondered, if the dice had not rolled out a seven, would I have sired any cane-cutters by Mollie? And could I ever have made a go of it in the sugar country? Hart's shrewd remarks acted on me like a surgeon's probe—one stab of pain, and the trouble was over and finished.

For several days we walked steadily west. At points, the track left the railroad, apparently for some outlying sheep station, and later it would reappear from somewhere. When there was no track we kept to the rail path, and where there was no path we stumped across the sleepers. The railroad led due west, and we were bound to stick to it. During the first two days we trudged through suburbs and little settlements indirectly connected with Rockhampton, and the people hereabouts were more disposed to set the dog at us than to help.

The food we had bought before setting out was soon used up, and by the third day we had nothing left at all. Then it was that we drew lots for the task of knocking at the door of some lonely little wood-and-iron dwelling, usually that of a rail worker, to ask for some woodchopping in return for food and water.

Being January, it was very hot. Hart became less immaculate. He shed his beautiful coat on the first day, and by the third his silk shirt was palpably soiled and his trousers the worse for sundry battles through patches of thistle. What he had left was his distinctiveness. Hart was always Hart and not just someone.

Ted, having no razor, developed a black bristle around his jaws which gave him an air of ferocity, while Hugh loped steadily along, singing happily, telling bawdy jokes, and sighing for the girls of Rockhampton. Myself, I managed as well as anyone.

We covered fifteen miles the first day, but only five the second, and then decided that ten miles a day was good humping. In that heat, it was. Each of us, right from the start, had his own private enemy, an army of about one hundred nasty little flies swarming around one's head, and no matter how many one killed the swarm never became any smaller.

Trains were quite an event. The passenger trains passed at the rate of one every three days each way, and the goods three or four times a week. The driver generally hailed us with his whistle, and there were times when the driver or some passenger threw a packet to us. It might be half a loaf or yesterday's newspaper. One thing was certain: they all knew, these lucky people hurtling along at fourteen miles an hour, that we weren't walking for fun, and they knew it wasn't easy.

We were in desperate straits when we fetched up, near sundown, at a small hut alongside the track. The plate-layer who lived there alone was overjoyed to see us, cooked us a fine meal with new hot bread and roast meat washed down with a gallon of strong milkless tea.

He had a pet goanna, which looked like a miniature crocodile, and told us it was much more reliable than a dog. It ran up a tree as we approached, and stayed there until we departed next day. We went off with full stomachs and the welcome information that we weren't far from a lumber camp.

"You might get work there," said the old boy, and added, "though I shouldn't reckon you would."

Nearing sundown we heard the shriek of the circular saws, and as we approached the noise ceased. We came into the camp just as the sawmill crews and the wagon-men were streaming across from their tents by the creek to the pub, vanishing through the swing halfdoors like a column of ants into a nest.

"I could drink a gallon without drawing breath," said Hugh, wiping his dry lips.

"Trouble is," said our thrifty Ted, "we can't afford both a meal *and* a pint."

"I'll see the boss," said Hart.

We dropped our loads on the verandah and walked in together. They looked a healthy happy well-fed crowd in the bar, having their first pint of the day with a good hard day's work behind. We must have looked to them like four scarecrows left too long in the field. But Hart made for the boss like the one hundred per cent world citizen he was.

"Good evening, boss," he said. His tone was friendly but not conceding.

The publican looked us over in one swift glance. "Evening, boys," he said. "What're you drinking?"

"Before we decide that," said Hart, without any inflection whatever, "I have to ask you how much is the meal."

The publican's eyes smiled. "Low as that?"

"Low as that," said Hart.

"I'll fix yez a meal and a pint each," said the publican. "Get washed and go into the dining room. I'll tell Marie."

Hart nodded and said: "Thanks." He beckoned us outside and led us down to the creek. "He's standing the meal and a pint," said Hart.

"When they're good," said Ted, "they're bloody good. My oath."

We had steak and eggs and liver, all piled up on the plate, with sweet potato and bread and butter, with cheese afterwards, a glorious spread taken with a pint of warm beer (no ice here). The publican came in while we were eating, had a word with his wife—asking her, I suspected, to be sure we had our bellies filled—and then came across to our table. "I don't suppose," he said, "none of youse blokes can hit the joanna."

"Bluey can."

"I'm not much good," I protested.

"And Ted here sings a fine song."

The publican nodded. "It gets a bit dull for the boys out here," he said, "and they get kinda irritable later on, at times. But whenever we can get a singsong goin' why, it's fine. I'd be obliged if you would ding it," he said to me. "Don't matter how bad it is, cobber."

Bad was the word. The sawmill boys wanted old Australian jingles I didn't know yet. One or two of them the whole world knew, but whenever someone came lurching over for a "special request" I had to call on Ted for something out of his Cockney repertoire. The beer flowed freely, and we staggered down to the creek for our night's camp very happy. The publican gave us breakfast which was exactly the same as the dinner without the sweet potatoes, gave us each a two-shilling piece, and his wife filled our tucker bags.

"Get west as far as you can," said the publican. "Farther you go, the more work and the better pay. No good around here." He leaned over, confidentially. "Whyn't you jump a train? Nobody humps the swag when there's trains around."

"I tried it once," I said, "and got fifteen days."

"Yes, but you hit the stationmaster," said Ted.

"You did?" The publican thumped the bar. "Hey, Marie!" he called to his wife, "Marie, the kid here got fifteen days for stoushing a stationmaster! Say, where was this?" I felt he was not merely approving, but was congratulating himself on having dished out a free welcome to the right types.

"Now don't you go getting into no more trouble like that," said the publican's wife, "or you'll end up just a swaggie with corks in your hat. I've seen 'em, boy."

"You'll hit the mount'ns soon," said the publican. "There's a track winds away to the north, but you'd best stick to the rails."

"It's dangerous if you don't know it," said Marie.

"They'll get through. Don't cross the bridges in the dark, boys. It's a long way to fall."

We shared out our tucker and our waterbags, swung up our swags and shuffled off, single file, along the narrow path below the sleeper ends, going west. There was no mistaking the direction, for the one pair of rails ribboned ahead as far as the eye could see. You could have put a spirit level on them at any time and the bubble would be dead centre.

The heat and dazzle of the sun came spinning upwards from the rails. The flies buzzed savagely without ceasing, and one's own salty sweat was a nuisance. Sometimes we talked, even argued about quite stupid matters. Sometimes we told stories. And sometimes we walked in a silence which was complete except for cursing the flies.

Mirages came and went. At first, they were exciting, believable. One saw, beside the tall trees with their reflections in the inevitable lake, the iron roofs and outlines of the substantial house and buildings of the owner of a big estate. It all melted into nothing as one approached.

Walking on the sleepers added to the irk and weariness of the journey, for the distance between sleepers was less than an ordinary pace, so that one travelled like a hobbled horse, with billycans banging and the waterbag spilling precious water.

Soon, we were making such poor progress that we decided to walk entirely by night and rest during the day. This meant finding shade and, if possible, a waterhole. Sometimes we found neither when daylight came, and had to stagger on.

Ted's boots gave trouble. One had to be bound to his foot with a piece of wire. Hart, though a near-blond, was now walking without a shirt. The sun had little effect on him whereas my arms and neck still burned raw, in my third tropical summer.

I wrote a letter home just before a sundown. "You should see the moon rise out here, Dad. It reminds me of a Welsh choir, can't say why. The sky is black, deep black, and against it the stars sparkle like white lights shining through cuts in a velvet curtain. They sparkle and twinkle as though they are alive. Indeed, I feel they really are alive. Then the moon comes up, very fast, enormous, bright as a new florin, and soon it is throwing long sharp-edged shadows across a bluish white country."

"Having a moan to yer Dad, Bluey?" asked Ted.

"Not a moan," I said. "Just explaining that we have to come west now to get more money together before we go back to the sugar."

"You're really going back to the sugar?"

"Ted, whatever we do, we've got to have some money. We've got to get regular work and save and save. Then it's easy."

"Easy! We don't even know how to grow sugar."

"Ted, you don't have to grow sugar. If you use your brains you can make a go of anything in this country. Just a bit of capital. Ted, you know what I've been thinking?"

"New idea for making a fortune?"

"I've been thinking that if you and I could start a store somewhere, we'd soon have a store in every town in Australia. It's wide open, Ted! Just think of the bush stores we've seen—piles of boundary riders' boots, dungarees, grey flannel singlets, tinned herrings, tea, flour and sugar and that's about the lot. Not a thing for a woman, Ted, not a luxury for anyone."

Ted peered about for the stump of fag he had carefully set down before sleeping. He was short-sighted.

"You ever kept a store, Bluey?"

"You know I never kept a store, but I'd bet I'd keep a better store than any store I've seen in the bush. I bet I'd have some good tobacco instead of that filthy plug you can't keep alight. I'd have scent and powder for the ladies. And

I'd have fruit, plenty of fruit. And vegetables up from the coast. I'd dress the shop and have a shop window. Why, they don't even bother about windows out here . . ."

"With natty gents' walking sticks and cummerbunds, and grand pianners and Persian carpets?"

I hated him when he sneered. I shut up. But he changed, quite surprisingly.

"I daresay, I daresay, Bluey. Any case, let me tell you you're dam lucky to have a mum and dad to write home to, whether you moan or not. And maybe to go home to one day. Bluey, I'm ten years older than you and life has nearly always been lousy for me. I expect that's why I'm a bloody pig sometimes.

"I had a father who was a son of a bitch——he never would tell me what happened to my mother. An aunt brought me up, and she didn't want the job either. I started work when I was eight, Bluey, just to get the odd penny for food——washing doorsteps, delivering newspapers, any bloody thing they let me do.

"I come out to Queensland, after I lost my job at the tram depot, because the emigration feller said nobody ever went hungry in this country. I told 'em I was a farm labourer and they give me a free passage, but I never saw a farm in my life. Nobody told me I'd make a fortune, but they did give me that yarn about free land and ten pounds an acre.

"We saw some of that land, you and me. I wonder how many get sucked in trying to work it? Covered with prickly pear twenty feet high. My God, what a hope! So we tried the sugar. I never seen no millionaires around the Proserpine, neither. I did see some rich Chinese, and plenty of flying foxes and snakes, and I worked my guts out for one and fourpence an hour in the mills, same as you, with a pound knocked off every week for tucker. Now we're humping it out west, hearing the same old yarns. It's always better the farther you go. Like them bleeding mirages."

I folded my letter away and started to get ready for the night's march.

"You make me feel I came from a rich family, Ted," I

107

said. "You know why I am always hoping to make a lot of money? My people are poor. They kept themselves poor spending every penny on the children. I was dead keen to come out here, and my old man gave in because he thought if I worked in London I'd be a consumptive.

"He's a dreamer, too, like me. He dreams I'm going to have a fine farm, with corn and cows and pigs and newlaid eggs, and lashings of grapes and peaches and oranges, just like the coloured pictures in the booklets they send you about Australia. He thinks I can do all that and he and Mum will be able to come out one day and take it easy on my farm.

"I can't tell him that I've seen the small cocky farmers, working eighteen hours a day, with all the family working too, and still hardly making a go of it. I can't tell him the dream is busted, Ted. But I still think this is the one country where any man can do well at *something*, if he gets stuck in. That's why I hang on to my hopes."

"You're dead right," said Ted. That made me feel a lot better, because I knew that if I'd have a go, so would he.

I gave Hart and Hugh a shake and came back to Ted. "Sometimes out here," I said, "I feel terribly lonely, and I say to myself that I'd gladly give a whole month's pay if I could stand for just one hour in Trafalgar Square, or outside the Mansion House, and watch all the people. Just stand and watch them all. Thousands and thousands of people in front of me, instead of one crow on a barbed wire fence."

The flies had gone, the mosquito hum had started, and we went off. Within a couple of hours the moon was up. I heard the voice of Hugh, who was leading some twenty yards away, talking to Hart: "My God, that blonde in Rockhampton . . ." His voice trailed away.

"I hope," Ted remarked gloomily, "my trunk is safe, back there in the left luggage in Rockhampton, until I can send for it. I don't trust those fellers."

"You don't trust anyone much, do you, Ted?"

Dumping Ted's brown tin trunk had been a joyous relief to me. His worldly possessions were in it, pretty well everything he had ever possessed, and nothing would persuade him to get rid of it. Getting around Brisbane, moving around the sugar country looking for work, wherever we went that trunk had to go.

We were now on an embankment, walking along a pair of duckboards each six inches wide down the centre of the rail track, shuffling along in moderate comfort. Ted was remarking that five miles would do him, what with one boot falling to pieces and his belly empty, when Hugh shouted from the front: "Hold it, boys."

For me, holding it meant dumping the lot.

"It's a bridge," said Hugh. "You'd better come and look at it."

Some thirty yards ahead, the earth seemed to have been split apart, leaving a ravine with sides almost vertical. The moonlight reflected from projecting ledges of stark rock, and one could see the outlines of boulders at the bottom, a long way down in the darkness. There was no sign of water. I had always had a fear of heights and stood well back, but Hugh stepped out along the duckboards quite briskly and came back saying, "It's quite good. The boards are still with us and there's a handrail on the left. Let's get moving."

Ted peered into the ravine. "Hell of a way down there," he muttered. "We're in rotten shape, I think we oughter wait till daylight. Maybe there's a road round this lot."

"A road?" Hugh burst into laughter. "We haven't seen a road for three days. This is a bit of fun, boys—breaks the monotony. Come out on the bridge and see for yourselves."

Ted and I walked a bit along the boarded track. Then I stopped and he went on. "Only one hand rail," he said, "and a lot of nothing on the other side. Even Blondin could see where he was going. A fine thing! They expect us to get out west to work and they don't even give us a road to walk on. What a bloody country!"

Hart had said nothing. Now he ended the discussion. "We know there is no other way," he said. "We've got hardly any food left, only a drop of water, and we're not fit to travel in the sun. So let's hitch our pants and start, and hope some unfortunate human being lives within the next five miles."

He picked up his gear. "You first, Hugh. Not too far ahead. Shout back as you go. The light's none too good. You next, Ted. You follow Ted, Bluey, and I'll be behind you. Right behind you, Bluey."

"We might climb down," said Ted, but he wasn't putting it forward as a proposition.

"You'd break your neck," said Hart.

"This could be suicide," Ted said as he adjusted his ill-made swag. "One slip and you'd be over the side. Or if the moon goes behind a cloud, or if a train comes when we're halfway. Sheer suicide."

"That's it exactly," said Hart. "Just a matter of taking the odds. All ready?" He turned to me. "You all right?"

"If you go, I go," I said, "but it's no use my pretending I'm good at this, because I'm terrified of heights."

"How terrified? Your head swims? You faint?"

"Not so bad as that. Just frightened to death. But I suppose it must be safe. I mean, they'd make it safe, wouldn't they? The government, I mean. After all, blokes like us have to get out there."

There was a brief reprieve while Ted's boot was strapped more firmly to his foot and then big Hugh yelled "Tallyho!" and started out across the bridge. He disdained the hand-rail, swung ahead and waited for us to get into motion.

Ted followed and I was next, holding the rail tightly as the track approached the edge of the ravine.

"Don't look down," said Hart quietly. "Take it easy. I'm right alongside, and if you do slip I'll look after you. But you won't slip, Bluey. Just swing along, Bluey. Swing along."

My attempt to swing along must have been pitiful. I was desperately afraid. This was a test I had never expected.

But Ted started talking. Queer, I thought, that a man's innermost secrets should just spill out of his mouth when he was crossing a dangerous bridge.

"Never would have been in this mess but for a woman," he said.

"A woman?"

"Foreman's wife at the tram depot. I was the lodger, she was a man-eater. But he was my pal. He gave me my job, got me my union ticket, helped me with overtime. But I was on night shift when he was on days, and when he went off to work she started messing around me. Why me? Well, I was there. And one day I up and told her she was a dirty bitch, and she blew up good and proper. Then my pal began to get peculiar and one day I was fired. Just like that. Fired and told to get out."

I was only half listening. Perhaps Ted talked to keep my mind off the ravine. Ted and Hart discussed the affair, and the perfidy of all women. It was all very interesting. Nevertheless, I looked down. The depth and danger had a fascination for me which was overpowering. I looked down, stopped and trembled.

We were now well out over the ravine, when Hugh announced: "No more handrail, chaps. But the boards are still with us."

No more handrail. On each side were the sleeper ends, and beyond them, black emptiness. I found myself calculating whether, if a man stumbled and slipped, he would have time to clutch a sleeper or a rail before going through the gap between the sleepers. Or suppose he went over sideways? People on circus trapezes could swing themselves up again quite easily—but could I? I was quite sure I could not.

There was some steel framework supporting each end of the bridge, and one could, I speculated, cling to it if the worst happened. But out in the middle of the bridge it was just sheer drop into the darkness down to the rocks. I found myself remembering the shuddering thrill I once felt at a circus when a man on a high wire, with nothing but an umbrella to aid his balance, pretended to slip.

We were halfway across when Hugh shouted back: "No more boards." He sounded quite cheerful about it. Instinctively I stopped, half hoping that this must mean turning back. But Hart, behind me, said: "Keep going, Bluey. Move a bit faster now."

He spoke quietly yet I knew I had to do it. So I trudged

steadily to the end of the boarding and then, in frantic haste to get it all over, I stumped hard from sleeper to sleeper with my eyes staring steadily on the lines.

We pulled up for a rest on the other side. "Not so difficult," Hugh remarked, "when you've got a load in each hand. I expect we'll meet some more of these ravines."

We did. Some bridges were quite short. Others, interminably long, and with neither handrail nor boards. I tried to persuade myself that I was getting used to it, sleeper-hopping over chasms, but in fact I was in a sheer funk the whole time. There were moments of near panic, as for instance when Hugh called, "Was that a train whistle?" The railroad was winding through cuttings and the sound of a whistle must mean the train was close. But no train came.

There was a moment when Ted's wire foot strapping hit a protruding dog spike. He staggered a few steps, fell to his knees without falling through, and was up again with a stream of Cockney curses which were new to me. It sounded like a wildcat spitting.

There was also a moment when Hugh, out in front, in the middle of a bridge, took it into his curly head to stop, put some of his gear on the sleeper he stood on, and let out an Australian "Cooee". He said he wanted to test the gorge for echoes. Now Hart was annoyed. "Don't stop, you fool!" he shouted. "Keep going! Keep moving!" There was a moment, too, when I stopped to brace my swag to ease the leather strap biting into my shoulder. Shifting the swag while standing on a single sleeper was difficult, so I stood sideways straddling two sleepers. It must have seemed to Hart that I was falling.

"Keep moving, Bluey," he said urgently. "Just forget you're on a bridge, kid."

"Yus, ferget yer on a bridge," said Ted. "We're on the ole Royal Sovereign going down to Margit. Ain't it grand! Let's all sing a song." He stumbled again and became quieter for a while. Then, as though he remembered something: "How're you going back there, Bluey? Not too bad after all, eh?"

"Bluey's doing fine," said Hart, for me. My clothes were

112

soaked with sweat. I had said several prayers and had become so benumbed with fear that I could tell myself I had a fifty-fifty chance of survival.

CHAPTER THIRTEEN

Hart splits the foursome

THE DAWN CAME, and with it the hot sun and the flies. We walked until we found shade—shade, but no water. There we flung our kit down.

"Get me some wood for a fire," I said. I was the party cook. They got a fire going while I unpacked and sorted what was left of our stock of food.

"What's to eat, Bluey?"

"One tin of soused herrings and no can opener, piece of cheese gone stale, tea and sugar for two days, no more tinned milk, some of the bread I made, piece of bacon not too healthy, and this lump of mutton which I'll have to chuck. Flies have got to it."

"Any cigarettes?" asked Ted.

"Three. One each for you."

"Well," said Hugh. "let's hope we're near Emerald. I could eat all that lot before starting on a good breakfast."

"You can have my share," said Ted, "if I have your cigarette."

"What we have to watch," said Hart, "is the water. Maybe we're all half a stone lighter than when we started, but it won't hurt us. Water—that means something. Tea we must have. Bluey, you share out all the food, but make enough tea for one mug each. If we don't find a waterhole tomorrow we could be in trouble."

"Keep the tea leaves," said Ted. "I've heard you can smoke 'em.'

We munched the stale scraps, drank the hot strong tea. Hugh yawned: "I'd give something for a quart of 3-X bitter from the barrel in my village pub."

"For me," said Ted, his gritty voice slightly husky, "I fancy a Woodbine with a cup of real tea with real milk and sugar out of a proper china mug like you get off a coffee stall in the Old Kent Road."

My thoughts didn't go back to the Old Country at all. I was thinking of an iced gingerbeer from a soda fountain in Mackay.

"There may be rain around," said Hart. "Let's get some sleep."

We were awakened by an ancient sundowner going east and he told us we were within nine miles of Emerald. He sat on his swag, handed us his stick of Yankee Doodle, each in turn, to cut off a chew (not one of us could rise to this yet) and offered to bake us some damper bread. My own damper now finished, had been yellow, mouldy and hard as a brick. We ate the old man's hot bread with gusto, while listening to his bush yarns, and continued along the track. "Best git there quick," said the old man. "Rain's comin'."

It came an hour before we hit Emerald. This was rain such as I had never seen, not even on the coast during the monsoons—tropical rain belting down at an inch per hour. We staggered through it blindly. If a train had come upon us we should have neither seen nor heard it.

Within the hour the country on either side of the track was aflood. It was cooling, swamping, deafening. We struggled through it for the last two miles of our journey, and then came to a fine broad road bridge—the bridge across a great ravine, the empty bed of a river. Empty an hour before, but fast filling up.

Across the bridge was Emerald, half a street, stores and pubs all on one side, the shady side. In front of us, facing the bridge, was a long low building. We staggered inside. It was a boathouse, containing two lifeboats. Astonishing sight.

A group of men sat around a fire cooking sausages. They looked up as we entered, four half-drowned newchums with boots flapping open and town clothes torn and sodden.

"Dump yer swags in the corner there, boys," said one, "and get some hot grub inside yez."

We never heard happier words. Stripping down to nothing, we sat steaming around the fire and ate steadily. The supply of sausages seemed inexhaustible. Nobody minded how much we ate. This always struck me as strange, for my family were poor and ate frugally. But here food was cheap, very cheap, and in the Queensland bush to give food meant no more than passing the time of the day.

"Why the boats?" asked Hugh presently.

"Floods," said an Australian. "If this rain doesn't stop within a few hours we'll have those two boats working full time pulling people out that creek."

But the rain ceased as suddenly as it had come. Next morning the sun shone with a hard golden glare, and having dried our clothes we stepped out into Emerald. There was enough money in the kitty for shilling breakfasts at one of the pubs—porridge, bacon, liver, chops, steak, bread, jam and coffee in abundance—and for cigarettes for Ted and tobacco for the other pair. Then, knowing by now our "rights" as travellers, we stepped round to the police house for our rations. Chits on the stores for flour, tea, sugar, meat, enough to last a week.

Emerald was hospitable. Mining folk called us from the swing doors of the pubs to come in for a drink, and this put us in a quandary. We couldn't pay our whack, yet we all knew by now the danger of refusing. It was resented. Hugh settled it by saying so simply and sincerely: "We're all dead broke, but we'll be glad to have a drink, by God."

Within an hour the whole of the drinking community of the handful of pubs in Emerald knew our history and was determined to buy us all we could handle. By now I could knock out a tune or two on Carlo's little accordion, and Ted was soon shattering the peace of this village with his tear-jerking sentimental songs. Hugh drank solidly. But Hart was elsewhere, busy making inquiries. The men of Emerald seemed to be making plenty of money, and he made it his business to find out how.

On the following morning, Hart said: "Boys, I think we'll have to split up for a while. They tell me there are sapphire diggings around here, but that it's very heavy work. I would like to try it, and so would Hugh. But I doubt if either of you two could manage it. I met a man last night who needs a couple of hands to complete the team starting on his diggings tomorrow." He added, as an afterthought:

"I couldn't talk him into taking you in. It just wasn't on."

There was silence when he stopped speaking. I was shocked that he made no semblance of apology for so obviously pushing us off immediately it suited him. I looked at the curly headed Hugh. He said nothing but, I felt, was both ashamed by Hart's bluntness yet too attracted by the proposition to refuse it.

It was Ted who broke the silence. He said: "Suits me. Suits me fine. How about you, Bluey?"

"Well, yes, I suppose so," I said. "There must be other chances for digging sapphires. I daresay we can find our own jobs."

"Don't try," said Hart incisively. "From what they tell me this is extremely tough and exhausting, and after what we've been through we may not be able to last long ourselves. It's a sheer gamble. One might hit a patch of sapphires tomorrow, or next year, or never in a life-time. You can have all the tucker, of course, and anything else we have. Write us at Emerald post office as soon as you get an address—we must keep in touch."

Within thirty minutes they had rolled out of Emerald for the diggings at Anakie, forty miles away.

"That was a bit sudden," I said. It was all I could think of saying. It didn't represent my sense of loss, of being deserted, betrayed in fact, as Hugh and Hart had stepped through the door from the cool dimness of the boathouse and strode into the glare of the Queensland sun.

We were an ill-assorted quartette, it was true, but we were all English, all struggling to live in and live with this hard country, and we had in a sense each taken an unspoken oath of loyalty to the foursome. Hugh, despite his selfishness, was a grand companion.

Hart! Well, Hart took my money in Brisbane. Hart would always use his friends. But Hart meant more to me than I could assess. He had the inflexible power to look life or death right in the eye and when that door shut behind him I felt utterly defenceless and without a clue to the future.

Ted smoked a cigarette thoughtfully, and his eyelids

closed to slits as he stared into the fire. "Hart," he said, "is not such a stinking bastard as he appears to be. It's just the way he puts things and does things. Them two blokes are fitter than us, Bluey. Hugh's fourteen stone of muscle and bone, and Hart looks to me like he's bin a champion athlete at something or other. Cold as a fish, but tough. The diggers wouldn't want us, but that's no reason why we should hold the others back. We won't starve, Bluey. Don't worry, I'll get a job pretty soon."

But the job fell to me, the same day. A bearded bushman leaning against a verandah post of a pub stopped me as we were passing.

"You want work?"

"Yes, we certainly do," I said.

He looked us over critically. "Only want one man. Three weeks' job. You," he said to me. "Ever done any well-sinking?"

I remembered the cue—never say you can't do a job. "That's a funny thing," I said, postponing the lie although I knew I'd have to tell it. "I've done quite a lot."

"Thirty shillings a week," he said. "Only one."

I shook my head. "Can't leave my cobber behind."

We argued a bit, but it was clear the old chap was anxious to get away, and before long he said: "He can come and cook for us. No wages."

We accepted. Thirty shillings a week with tucker was the highest pay either of us had ever had in the bush. True, Ted couldn't cook a piece of toast. He couldn't even shave himself. But that, we considered as we went over to the boathouse for our gear, would sort itself out. Any way you looked at it, we were better off.

The old selector came round on his horse. He took up both our swags, and off he went. A hundred yards from the end pub of Emerald and you were in country as wild as anywhere on the continent. We followed an old cockatoo fence through close scrub, the horse picking its own track while we stumbled along behind. We travelled northward steadily. With a horse as pacemaker you have to make a good stride.

"You making a fortune out of your selection?" I asked the old man. "We're interested, you know, because when we've earned enough money we're going to put it into something of our own, and I suppose it could be a selection."

"That a fact," said the selector. I thought he sounded just slightly amused. "It's not easy to get, a selection. I was born around here, and I've never been away more'n fifty miles in my life. It's all the same, they tell me. Except the sea. I'll see the sea one day.

"Every year the government has a ballot for land falling in on leasehold, cut up into selections. I've been in every ballot for more'n twenty years, until last year I was lucky. I drew this lot. Forty thousand acres. Not much, but it's mine!" He said that with deep satisfaction. "It's mine. I rent it from the government on a long lease. Ha'penny an acre a year, and dear at that. But it's mine!"

"You must have a lot of sheep or cattle on all that land?"

"You want to know what my stock is? Two horses, one dawg, ninety goats. You know why? No water. Not a drop. That's what they thought. But I been pokin' along the dry crick beds—you have to know the way water runs in these parts. That's why we're sinking this well."

"You've really struck water?"

" 'Bout two feet down."

"My word, that's fine!' I said. "Now you will make a fortune."

"Fortune?" The old selector looked ahead through the tops of the gums to the blue sky in the north. "I'll make a living, renting the scrubland and the waterhole to cattle drovers and sheepmen passing down to the coast. Maybe I'll make enough to build a real house. And maybe I'll marry. Who knows?

"Boy, unless you're born on land like this you can't understand that the only thing in life is to have land, your own land. Now, at last, I have mine, forty thousand acres of scrub. Here it is, we're on it now, have been these past two miles. With my own hands I can clear it, if I want, and now I have water I can start cattle. I can grow my own

119

food, my own meat. I can fence it, dig it, ride all over it, watch it develop and change. Didn't you ever feel like that about anything?"

"Certainly I did," I said, warmed by his sudden emotion. "My cobber and me, we both feel that way, don't we, Ted?"

"I could feel like that," said Ted, "if I had something of me own, like a slap-up fried fish shop at the Elephant and Castle. That could make a fortune."

"Fortune, fortune," murmured the old selector. "What's a fortune? What do you do with it? Yes, I've got a fortune —I'll show you it when we hit camp."

Camp was a lean-to—corrugated iron sheets making three sides and a roof, leaning against a great tree. The galley stood outside. Darkness was falling as the selector climbed down and unsaddled. Then he lit a lamp, and set the tea billy over some sticks thrown on hot ashes.

"This is my home," he said. A bunk stood against one side of the lean-to, a canned meat box at the head. There was no other furniture except some roughly cut bookshelves, on which there were two or three hundred books.

"And this is my fortune," said the selector, holding the carbide lamp high. I read the titles—Shakespeare, Cobden, Cowper, Swift, classics translated from Russian novelists and German philosophers, and a large number of Latin and Greek classics.

"Where do we sleep?" asked Ted.

"Oh, anywhere. Under a bush, I'd say. Heavy dews sometimes."

"You read these?" I asked. "Greek and Latin, too?"

"I taught myself," said the old man. He was trying to conceal his pride. "Never went to school—wasn't any school around here when I was a kid. Want me to translate some? Maybe tomorrow night, eh? Youse blokes must be tired."

"Under a bleeden bush," muttered Ted as he threw off his boots. "No wonder they want us to come out here. Blind old Riley, they really need people in these parts."

We lasted a week, at the end of which the selector wrote

out a cheque for one pound ten shillings and handed it to me.

"Never really thought you'd be much good," he admitted, "but you're stronger than I thought. Wanted you for company as much as anything, especially while we were finding the water. Wanted to share the sight with someone. Know what I mean?"

"I think so," I said. "And I'm sorry I'm not much good at well-sinking."

"Well, that and the fact that your cobber couldn't even catch a goat, and when I caught it for him he didn't even know how to kill it and skin it."

"How the hell would I know that?" roared Ted. "Never even seen a goat, so far as I know. You want a butcher, say you want a butcher. I ain't no butcher."

"Anyway, we've got the thirty bob," I said, as we struck the path southward towards the rail track. "And the old man's got his puddle hole."

"Thirty bob," he snorted. "Twenty-five mile out to this 'ere crazy goat farm and twenty-five mile back agin. 'Struth!"

"But," I pointed out, "we do have thirty bob, Ted, and we're going west together. Don't forget that. I reckon we'll do pretty well on our own, once we get you those new boots."

CHAPTER FOURTEEN

Hot words about LloyGeorge

A WEEK LATER, Ted with new boots, both of us with a good square pub meal inside, we were humping along the track, one each side of the rails. Low cloud shut us in, with its steamy heat compressing against the metals. The flies were biting with reckless venom and we trudged in silence, irritated, sweaty, bored, fatigued.

We were also hungry and thirsty. I was always the cook on our swag-humps; perhaps because I had picked up some clues to bush cooking from Snowy, the cook in the Narrabri country of New South. Not many clues, but a rough idea of making damper bread with flour, soda and cream of tartar, and knocking up scones and johnny cakes.

Experience taught me to hide salt, tea and sugar from the ants in close-lidded tins. I tried to take along an onion or two for the stew and even some butter on one occasion. But inevitably after the first few hours of a walkabout the job became one of concentrating on a never-ceasing fight against the ants.

The flies and mosquitoes were an irritant, but the ants were the curse of all who lived in the bush. They came in several sizes, colours and varieties. One had only to sit down for a couple of minutes' rest in the shade and the ants were attacking in columns. They adopted smothering tactics on reaching their objective, spreading out to march into everything at once. Food, every sort of ant quickly found and rendered inedible. The greenish black ant, known throughout the bush as the "pissant", had an unfortunate habit of falling into one's tea, and a single tiny "pissant" in a quart billy of tea rendered that tea foul-tasting beyond belief.

There were the slightly larger brown ants which sought out the inside of one's trousers. The moment their presence was detected, usually behind the knee or in one's crotch, they attacked, leaving a painful swelling. Larger and more ferocious varieties were the soldier ant and the big red fellow, three-quarters of an inch long, known as the bull-dog ant.

In dwellings, the legs of tables and food safes always stood in tins filled with water, and bush citizens had learnt to steep the buried part of the wooden piles in creosote and concrete to ward off the white ants which would otherwise eat steadily inside sawn timber unseen until one day the building collapsed.

Ants, it was admitted by bush folk, were nature's scavengers. They left the skeleton clean and tidy after the dingoes and the crows had finished with it, and without them possibly there could have been fevers and poisoning, neither of which I ever saw. Given fresh water and meat one would never be ill in the bush, barring accidents. Water and meat and—for the civilised—flour, tea, sugar and salt.

But whenever we met some grizzled old sundowner on the track it was amazing to perceive his collection of food-stuffs, as well as needles, threads, buttons and sundry implements. We were greeted once by a turbaned Indian, who insisted on making a curry for us. He produced all the ingredients, including some coconut.

Nevertheless, despite Snowy's tuition, and my attempts to keep our stock of food in good condition, our meals were invariably ghastly. Sheer hunger forced us, at times, to eat yellow-streaked damper, one day old but hard and cracking, dry and mouldy. Meat we had to eat as quickly as possible.

I used to have thoughts of catching a rabbit or some other wild creature and cooking it in hot ashes, native style, but we had no bushcraft whatever and when once we hooked a couple of herring-size yellow-belly in a little billabong with a piece of stale meat fixed on bent wire we concluded that this succulent triumph had been possible only because the fish were even more ignorant of the game than we were.

Such miracles apart, we ate well when we were able to buy or beg some food or draw our legal ration, and semi-starved on my cooking until the luck turned our way again. Ted pointed out gloomily on one occasion: "It must be only a matter of time before we throw the bleedin' seven."

Still, often scraggy and not too strong, we survived the shortage of food and the curse of the ants, which left us with the flies, the mosquitoes and a perpetual thirst.

"Flies!" exclaimed Ted. "Gor strike me bleeden hooray, I never known nothing like it. What do they live on when we ain't 'ere?"

"I suppose we ought not to talk," I said, "as we're right out of water."

"Sure to be a tank or something."

"Well," I said, "I've been meaning to discuss something with you for a day or two. You remember me saying what a chance there was out here for a real house-builder? That's what it's about. If we could only get a factory and make wooden houses that could be packed up and put on trains and wagons and easily nailed up—after all, the houses out here are very simple. No plumbing, no lighting, no water laid on. Just two rooms and a verandah."

"Oh, dry up," he growled.

Offended, I shut up. We covered a mile in silence. Ahead was the inevitable mirage. It looked beautiful. The hot blue rails ribboned dead flat across the plain into the Queensland haze, and the suffocating clouds sank lower.

"Bluey," Ted broke the silence at last, "your old man not a socialist, I don't suppose? Tory, probly?"

"My father," I said, still offended, "happens to be a Liberal, and so am I, if it interests you."

To my surprise Ted was nettled. "Liberal—huh!" No mistaking his contempt. "Middle-roaders and free-traders —never get you anywhere. All the Tory mob are crooked. They own the land and the banks and they bleeden well mean to keep 'em. But you know where you are with Tories. But the Liberals, a lotter wishy-washy tuppn'y ha'pny ninnies with their yappin' about three acres and a cow. Blimey, you kin 'ave the Liberals."

"And what's the matter with three acres and a cow? I bet you wish you had three acres and a cow in England now! You wouldn't have had to come out here if they'd let Lloyd George give us all three acres and a cow. One of the finest measures . . ."

He laughed angrily. "You're too young to unnerstand. You don't wanner try to argue about politics with a man like me. I'm not only ten years older but I've studied it all. I know it all. I know all these bleeden swindles of the politicians. I rumbled old LloyGeorge years ago."

We were both slightly mad with the heat and the flies. "You rumbled nothing, you bloody ignoramus," I threw at him.

"Well, blimey," he said softly. "He's actually swearin'. Good job his ole man didnt 'ear that."

"You leave my old man out of it, you snivelling know-all." I was in some difficulty, with a parched throat and having lost control through anger. "As a matter of statistics there's no reason at all why we couldn't all have three acres and a cow, and with plenty to spare. No reason at all."

I had fallen right into it, of course. "No reason at all, eh? Well, let me tell you any schoolkid who kin add up to ten kin work it out for hisself that there just ain't all them cows nor there ain't all them acres."

"I don't want to argue with you," I croaked at him. "It's a waste of breath. You're only a socialist, so you don't know any better."

Something in this remark at last got under Ted's skin. No doubt, too, the sweat was smarting his eyes and hunger gnawed at his stomach—for that's how it was with me on the other side of the track.

"You long skinny ass," he snarled. "You don't even know how many people there are in the United Kingdom."

"Oh, yes I do. Forty million."

"Forty-two," he said. "And 'ow many acres?"

"All I know," I blustered, "is that it's a fact and I've got a book at home to prove it."

"You got a book at 'ome," he sneered. "I don't need no books. I know. There's sixty million acres, so how can we

125

all have three acres each?"

No answer from me.

"What's more, s'pose we all 'ad a cow each? Who's goin' ter drink all the milk and eat all the cream and butter and cheese and all the beef from the bullocks? We'd all be tryin' to sell milk and no one wouldn't 'ave no money to buy it. Just a damn silly election swindle, a Liberal one."

"You look to me as if you could do with some of that milk and cream now," I said. "It's people like you with crazy ideas about socialism and sharing everything out who give us a bad name. My old man told the socialists where to get off. Everybody knows the socialists are all mad. Mad and lazy."

At that he stopped. As he glared short-sightedly across the hot rails he looked more like a frill lizard than ever, horrible and frightening, if harmless.

"You callin' me lazy?"

I was too far gone to care. "Yes I am!" I yelled back, recklessly ignoring the showdown that was obviously coming. "You leave me all the cooking, and the biggest load to carry. You can't even make a fire or shave your bloody self. You're just a lazy stupid socialist."

"Why, for two pins I'd smash your face in." His voice was husky, with emotion and with dust. His throat, too, was dry.

"You'd smash my face in!" I jeered. "I'd like to see you do it. I'm ready whenever you are."

This was calling him. Incidentally, it was probably my last boyhood approach to a crisis. He glared at me and wiped his sweaty face with his arm. "Only a bleeden lunatic would fight in this 'ere sun. We'll wait till we get to shade and water. Then I'll give you the biggest hidin' you ever 'ad in your young life."

He gave his swag a heave, changed his billycan and waterbag from one hand to the other, and shuffled away. I stared after him, my own anger oozing rapidly. We were both hysterical. Still—"All right," I called after him. "Soon as we get to some shade." And I, too, gave my swag a hitch and stumbled forward along the sleeper track once more. I

126

tried to swallow the choking dryness and vomited.

For a full hour we dragged ourselves alongside the hot blue metals without a word. He kept slightly ahead, and there was something about the movement of his scraggy body, a grim determination in his uneven walk, which expressed his implacable anger. I would have liked to talk if only to break the aloneness and take my mind off our desperate state—no water, no food, and no knowledge of how far we were from anywhere.

I wondered a bit about the fight, though the flies and my own near-exhaustion made impossible any mental concentration. But I did remember that I had boxed a bit, even though I had never really hurt anyone. So far as I knew Ted had never boxed. Physically, Ted wasn't tough. He was much older and he could talk fiercely. But in anger, I estimated, he was just a frill lizard.

Long before the end of that hour I badly wanted to drop down on the hot flints and rest. But I knew we dared not stop. Ahead the mirage vanished. The track began to climb a slight gradient: it seemed like a mountain to me. Now there was a cutting ahead, through which the track ran, winding slightly. A mile further on, across the plain, I could see a solitary leafless tree. I could have bet odds there was a crow balancing awkwardly on a branch squawking hungrily.

The sight of that dry plain scared me. We had been told we would strike a running creek by last nightfall, but we had seen no water. We had no food. There were times when one felt one could never go hungry in Australia, so rich was its natural bounty. And there were others, out here in the western plains, when one realised how desperately close one might be to death from starvation or thirst.

Now came the crows, a dozen of them flying towards us from that old dead tree. Horribly sinister, speculating as they flew in a ragged mob on their prospects of feeding off the human meat struggling along so slowly that surely they must drop within the next mile or two.

I was comforted a little by the presence just ahead of the dark little man who was really my pal. But I couldn't ask him to stop. Resting now might be the end. Staggering along, hoping something would turn up, just had to be done.

"Bloody bastards," I shouted at the crows but couldn't hear my own voice. I wondered whether I would go back home if I managed to get out of this spot alive, but I knew I'd asked myself that question before. I tried to forget where I was, tried to fill my mind with pictures of the mulberry tree at school, of outings to Epping Forest, of my half of a bedroom at home, of Sunday dinner, nearly always roast beef, Yorkshire pudding and a heap of cabbage and potatoes, sometimes parsnips and carrots.

But I had to give up the attempt. To forget the flies and the crows, the oppressive heat, the ache of limbs and the pain in my left shoulder where the swag strap was biting, above all the parchedness from cracked lips right down to the pit of my stomach, to blot out all this could mean only one thing. Collapse.

There came the question, how far could we go? The dead tree looked even farther off now. But it became a target in my mind. Whatever might happen afterwards, one would get to that tree. I tried counting paces, making each hundred a target. "I'll get another hundred anyway." Then—"Maybe if I can do that five times . . ."

Then I noticed that Ted was no longer trudging with shoulders and head bent downwards: he was actually looking up, looking ahead, and his pace had quickened. I wiped the sweat from my eyes. Now I could see, just beyond the old tree, the faint outlines of a large square tank, its grey sides almost merging with the greyness of the plain beyond.

This must surely be the miracle, the saving miracle. Unless it was a mirage. Could there be a tank mirage? Did it depend on whether one was half conscious, or half crazed? Bush mad? I made a great effort and managed to get alongside my old mate, and together we stumbled forward, one on either side of the rails, as the outlines of the tank became sharper, real. It was a tank, a water tank, a reserve for the locomotives.

There was the whistle of an engine some way behind us,

but neither of us bothered to look back. It would be the goods that went through three times a week—no passengers to throw us food. It was water we wanted. Water would save us from the crows. We dropped everything in a pile and made for the tank. It stood four or five feet high, and there was no covering plate over the large hole in the top.

"Must have a drink," I said unnecessarily, and felt my lip split open.

Ted muttered ironically: "No shade 'ere," and unhooked his pannikin. He plunged his arm through the hole. The pannikin came out empty. We looked inside together, and the hot breath from the dry flaking interior was stifling, sickening. The metal was at blister heat.

We looked at each other. In Ted's eyes I saw the mounting realisation of what it meant. No water. It wasn't exactly fear that I saw; rather, a grim understanding that we were beaten.

"It can't be," I whispered. But it was.

The goods train was chugging towards us, and stopped with a clatter and rattle as the trucks shouldered off the impact each against the next down the line. The burly engine driver leaned from his cab and shouted at us, pointing and waving us away.

"Take a runnin' jump," Ted shouted back.

The train started off again with its bumps and clatter, and then pulled up with a screech. This time it was the guard who opened his door and shouted.

"Come on, you bastards," he called angrily. "You want to go somewheres, don't youse?"

We stared at him for a moment. "Gorblimey," muttered Ted. "A lift! They're givin' us a lift! In a bleedin' train!"

Grabbing cans and bundles we staggered over to the train. The guard threw open the door of one of two passenger compartments attached to his own.

"Where d'you wanter get?"

"Where there's work," said Ted. "Some town out there. Don't matter where."

"Get in," said the guard, irritably. "I'm locking the door.

129

Pull down them blinds. This ain't allowed, carrying swaggies."

Ted said it. "Ain't got a dropper water, old sport?"

"Youse newchums," growled the guard. "Whyn't you bring yer nurses?" He climbed into his own cabin and reappeared and thrust into my hands a can of cold tea. Still cursing, he came back again with a hunk of salt beef, two loaves and a tin of jam. "And keep quiet when we stop," he threatened. "This ain't allowed."

He waved his arm and the goods jerked violently and eased into a smart fourteen miles an hour . . .

Fifteen minutes later Ted let up a blind and read the label on the jam tin. "Pineapple and ginger," he said suspiciously. "What muck these Australians eat."

"Pineapple and ginger! Man, that's lovely grub," I said. "But how are we going to open the tin, old cobber?"

Ted's little eyes smiled into mine. "I'll open this 'ere bleedin' tin," he promised, "if I 'ave to do it wiv me teef."

I stretched full length on the cushioned seat. It was comparatively cool, and there were no flies. My once white skin was scorched and cracking and my limbs were sore. But my stomach was comfortably full, my thirst forgotten, my fears away in the limbo of the past.

Ted said: "And I thought that driver was givin' us the works fer touching the railway tank. G'blimey, y' never know in this country, blowed if you do."

Lloyd George was never mentioned between us again. He, too, had drifted into the forgotten past. There was always a future ahead of one in Australia; one could always start from scratch again. The past never mattered.

I awoke hours later as we bumped to a halt. There was silence. Cautiously I raised a blind. It was night. Feet crunched along the metal and a voice said: "Got any jumpers aboard, guard?"

"No."

"Sure? Better look. Very strict jess now about swaggies hopping the trains."

Ted sat up. I could just make out his form in the dark-

130

ness. I leaned across the carriage and whispered to him to hush.

There was a hand on the door handle. "Carriages are locked," said the guard. "No passengers this trip. Let's try the closed wagons. I know where the bastards hide up."

"Good-oh," said the other voice. The feet crunched away. Doors banged. The guard shouted. At long last the driver blew a blast on his whistle and we were off again.

How long we travelled neither of us could tell, for we did not carry watches. The train pulled up, our carriage door was unlocked, and the guard said: "This is it, new-boys. Can't get you any further. Hop down quick."

We gathered our collection of pans and cans and swags and climbed down into the sunshine. I looked around and saw just bush. Open bush country, flat as a cricket pitch, but clothed with strong, greyish Mitchell grass and dotted with broad gums and twisted ironbarks. Half a dozen big birds wheeled and hung in the sky; apparently nothing moved below.

We asked where we were.

"Five or six miles from Barcaldine, which is as far as we go. Can't take you into the station."

We were abjectly profuse in thanking him. He looked embarrassed and waved his hand to the driver to get on again.

"Thank him, too," I said, "and if we see you there we'd like to stand a couple of pints."

He almost smiled as his van passed us.

"Funny thing," said Ted as he combed his hair. "God, I need a shave. Funny thing, that guard was a real decent bloke but he just hated to have it mentioned. He chances his job to help a couple of helpless stragglers from the Old Country, and I bet he'd do the same thing for any other swaggie, and to hell with the Queensland government. But if some sharp spieler tried to jump his train he'd chuck him off over a bridge. That don't make sense in England. At home, a guard's a guard, and regulations is regulations. Here, a guard's just a bloke like us, with a flag."

We came into Barcaldine on a good bush road. Once, in

fact, we saw a motor car—still a rare sight in central Queensland. Transport, apart from humping the swag, was ninety-eight per cent by saddle horse or buggy, with the odd car and the beginning of a motor bike fashion among the higher-paid travellers, such as shearers and wool-classers. Roads were just tracks and became difficult for wheeled vehicles of any weight when it rained. But it seldom rained.

We liked Barcaldine at first glimpse. There, along the road on the south side of the station, were several hotels. Some—the swank places—were two-deckers with iron balconies. We mooched past five pubs, and at the fifth the publican was whistling cheerily as he swept some rubbish away from his doors. He looked up at us with a greeting not possible to resist.

"You got a room?"

"Come in."

He bought us drinks on himself, which left us on the spot.

"I have to go to the post office," I said, "to get money. Can't buy a drink till then. We've come a long way."

So he produced the slate and we chalked up two more rounds and a good feed. Everything was looking up. The town was grand—laid out in the usual pattern of squares, but the neat little houses looked shady and prosperous and their gardens were bright and gay, and the purple clusters of dates looked luscious.

We each had a secret horde of savings, upon which we drew as frugally as possible. But by the evening Ted was shaved and dressed in new shirt and strides, and my ginger mop was cut and I also sported some new clobber. We felt we looked good, as we paid our week's board, one pound each, to the boss, Alec. That evening we wrote letters. We asked for mail to be forwarded, and we wrote to Hugh and Hart.

I also wrote home. Barcaldine (I wrote) is the most wonderful bush town I have ever seen. We both feel absolutely grand, and I think it must be the bracing air out here. There's a huge outdoor swimming bath—no roof on it—and the water's always warm because the bath's being fed all the time, day and night, by artesian bore. Down in the town there's a roller-skating rink! Isn't that amazing? And a moving picture house. We already know the bloke who plays the piano at the moving pictures and he says he can get us free seats for all the shows . . .

Better still, there was quite a prospect of work. Shearing in the sheds on a circuit could mean five or six months' work. Out of shearing season the big stations were often wanting teams for such jobs as fencing and ringbarking. There was always well-paid work, we were told, for drivers who could handle teams of bullocks or horses on the wool-wagon columns across the great spaces from the distant sheeplands into the railheads. Neither of us could drive a donkey, but we would never have admitted it.

Within a week, mail and parcels arrived; and here was one large and heavy parcel for me from the Old Country. We took it to our room and opened it. A letter from my mother fell out of the box as we took off the lid. Inside the box were packets of chocolate, a home-made cake, and a tin of Christmas pudding. It had arrived in Australia on Christmas Eve, several weeks ago, but the temperature was still over a hundred in the shade at Barcaldine.

"We'll eat the chocolate today," I said, "and keep the cake and the Christmas pudding until tomorrow."

The chocolate was a disappointment. It ran out of the packets as we opened them. On the following afternoon we went to our room. It was too hot for anything but rest. I was eager to get at the pudding, and this was no easy task, for the tin was heavily made and we had no can opener. It took an hour to make a jagged cut sufficient to wrench off the top, and here was our second shock: the pudding ran out of the can.

"Still," said Ted, being quite nice about the whole thing, "we have the cake and that looks solid."

It was solid. When my mother baked a cake it was well and truly baked. This one had been double baked during the two-month journey across the world. That wasn't important to wanderers who had learnt to eat and enjoy

133

anything the stomach did not absolutely reject. But English home-made cake, rich and heavy and cooked with the object of quelling fierce appetites on cold days, had no appeal to the taste buds here in the tropical bush. We fingered a few crumbs. Neither of us cared to state the truth, which was simply that we didn't want it.

So the eating of the cake was postponed, and the cake put back into the box with the can of runny pudding and the runny packets of chocolate, the box was pushed under the wardrobe and remained there until one hot night when I took it out and wandered along the road leading from town until I met an Aboriginal woman. To her I presented the box and wished her a happy birthday. She grabbed it and rushed away with her prize.

I walked back happily. It was a good country here in the outback, and as I flexed my muscles I felt strong enough, man enough now, to face anything. Maybe at last I had found the corner of Australia where I could earn and save, earn and save, grow in physique, grow in my knowledge of Australia and Australians and work towards the creation of something. Well, maybe.

Billy the pianist was the first of Barcaldine's characters whom we met. Billy was from "down Melb'ne way" and like most permanent inhabitants of bush pubs he never said why he had come out to the bush to live and never referred to his life before Barcaldine. His reason for this marooned existence could be any one of two: women or the law. No one would ever ask him which.

He was short, stumpy, fortyish, thinning on top, with the supple fingers of a card player or musician, and his life's target appeared to be to avoid any serious form of work. We found Billy a jolly companion, quite inoffensive, even charming, a steady drinker who never got drunk, and altogether one hundred per cent untypical Australian of the period.

There was a sensational American motion picture serial running at the little hall which served as a cinema. The programme was changed twice a week, which allowed just enough running time for the whole of Barcaldine to pack into the sessions, each of which left us gasping with excited speculation. We invariably left the lady at the point of death in some astounding predicament. She was beautiful and busty, brave but feminine, much desired but modest as a Sunday school teacher.

Billy had the music all in his head, for the serial and for the Keystone cops. "Moonlight Sonata" for the tender love scene, Wagner thumped out during the punch-ups, a piece of Bach dribbling along when the lady was riding blissfully through the Hollywood scenery.

Billy's control of five or six snatches of classical music was considered very high class. He could produce quite a dramatic effect on us by switching from the middle of a bar of gentle Bach to a double-fisted crash on the base keys when for instance the lady's horse reared at the ghastly confrontation of a swinging corpse. During the comedies Billy was nicely refrained. He had some quiet, unidentifiable music played so that we could laugh loudly without upsetting him and could even read the captions.

The repertoire never varied, but Billy always played his act, as it were, with professional aplomb, always received an ovation for his overture for which he bowed and showed the bald part of his skull, and completed the session with a powerful and thrilling "God Save the King" which sent us reeling into the fresh air filled with loyalty and imperial spirit.

Billy introduced himself to us while we were watching a game of poker. I had a head for cards, an instinct for the mathematical odds, and was saved from joining a bunch of shrewd professionals by the chubby pianist at my elbow: "Play auction, cobber?"

Ted and I had perfected an understanding as auction bridge partners down in the sugar country and regarded it as a minor source of income. The game was sweeping the cities and the backblocks.

Billy introduced us to his pal. "Best roller skater in Australia. Prob'ly in the world."

We shook hands with the handsome young celebrity, to his surprise. Shaking hands in the bush was a custom reserved for the prelude to an arranged fight, though most fights I had seen had no prelude at all.

"Can't see where the money is in being a skating champ," said Ted as we cut for deal.

Billy and the champ exchanged glances. "In a coupla munce," said Billy mysteriously, "when it's cooler, we'll be in the middle of it. Sacks of it."

"We? You a skater too?"

"Me," said Billy, "I'm Pete's manager. My deal. Spades."

We took eight shillings each from them, which was a day's pay on AWU scale, and won considerable respect. "There's a coupla shearers at the Royal," said Billy, "who call themselves the auction champs. They play for big money. You'd be a fair bet to knock 'em over, I reckon."

"We don't have big money," retorted Ted. "In fact we don't have much money at all."

"What you boys want," said the genial Billy, "is a manager. I'll fix the match. You bet what you want and I'll get the rest on. Leave it to me."

As the best player of the four I pointed out that anyone could win with aces and kings, and bad cards could beat any amount of skill. By now we were getting really pally. Billy gave us tickets for the picture show and Pete invited us to the skating rink to watch him train.

Pete trained every late afternoon and all day Saturdays. The rink was filled with girls, men too, watching and admiring the beauty of his action, the ease and audacity of his tricks. They skated with him and against him, and applauded him. Roller skating was a world vogue and Pete was all-Australian champion, Billy said.

"Training for some match?" asked Ted.

Billy shook his head. "Secret. Everybody wants to know what he's training for, and when I tell 'em it'll be a world sensation. You boys be around in two munce time. I shall want blokes I can trust."

"We gotter work," said Ted. "Soon."

"Boys," whispered the pianist, "this is going to make a fortune. Don't worry about work. I know. I seen it all happen in Melb'ne."

"But this ain't Melbourne," Ted pointed out.

"Don't make no difference," said Billy. He made a great flourish with a huge bath towel as he flung it over Pete's sweating shoulders and led him to the shower, amid applause from the Barcaldine fans. "Don't make no difference. Melb'ne, Sydney, Barcaldine, even down b' the crick."

CHAPTER FIFTEEN
Sunday morning in the stockyard

OLD MICK RYAN of Barcaldine had never expected to do any more serious ring fighting, and why should he? He was nearer fifty than forty. He'd been middleweight champion of All Western Queensland for five-and-twenty years, in which time he had flattened all comers in All Western Queensland and had been flattened every time he ventured against a boxer from the coast.

For the past ten years old Mick had reigned unchallenged, and now some upstart gold washer from Clermont had written to the papers claiming the championship. So here it was, all fixed, and old Mick was guaranteed ten pounds as his end, which was corn in Egypt they said, to a bloke who had to rely for free beer on a somewhat rusty reputation.

So Mick had gone into training. Every morning he went to the open air baths for a bit of exercising and sparring, and anyone was free to go along and take a clout from him.

That was how I got into the fight game. I went along, gaped and worshipped. It was fascinating to see the hairy old warrior work his man with a nice left until the position was exactly timed for the right hook which finished off the volunteer sparring partner. One morning only one volunteer turned up. The champ let his right go sooner than intended, and the spar lasted a few seconds.

That was when he turned to me, in despair. "Give us a workout, pal," he said. So I climbed out of the pool, dried, and proudly put on the big gloves. After that I had my two or three breathless, exciting rounds every morning.

Once old Mick knocked me into the pool accidentally, and immediately threw off his gloves, dived in and helped me out, full of apology. "He's a nice kid," he explained to a bystander, as I shook myself, "but I have to be careful not to stoush 'im properly. I don't want no trouble with inquests."

It was a bit of fun for him, all the same. He enjoyed showing me the straight left, the right counter, the old one-two and the secrets of footwork, and he gave me breathing exercises to improve my wind.

"A man's gotter be able to fight," he said to me one day, "or he ain't nothing. That's righto, Bluey?"

I agreed it was righto and the straight dinkum. I was desperately keen to learn to box, and I fancy I was picking up the theory and the science. But fighting is a two-way game, and although I was allowed to bash with all I could give, very seldom did I get hurt. The old scrapper was gentle. Too gentle.

Looking back, it is quite obvious that I wasn't the fighting type. I didn't have the killer instinct, the lust to hurt. Over this boxing business I was deceiving myself and the old pug encouraged the deceit. So I began to throw out my chest—not aggressively, but in a very confident manner. That's how I suddenly found myself right in the centre of the fight game.

There was an argument outside our pub about a bicycle pump. A kid I knew as Joe had a bicycle, and attached to it was an excellent pump. Pumps were vital out in the west, for if your pump was broken or missing you would have to send money down to the coast for a new one. Joe was being accused of stealing the pump by a hard-faced, broad-shouldered little tough called Stevens. An ex-jockey, they said. He was threatening to knock Joe's block off.

It could have been anyone's pump. What mattered to me was that Joe was a kid, and he was someone I knew, and I felt righteously indignant to hear young Joe being called a thieving bastard and threatened with murder. So I stepped right into trouble and stated, with the severity of an army sergeant: "Buzz off, you. That pump belongs to Joe, and Joe's a friend of mine. See?"

Stevens was a man of few words. He looked me over rapidly. Instinct shouted within me to prepare for immediate action. In short, I was in a fight.

The local cop approached rapidly from the back of the pub. His timing was exact to the second. "I don't allow street fighting," he said, wiping his mouth. He seemed to be accusing me. "You two want to fight. There's one time and place in this town, and that's Sunday morning at eleven o'clock in the stockyard."

"Suits me," said Stevens, menacingly.

"Suits me," I said, as nonchalantly as I could make it sound. But who can be anything but excited over his first real fight?

News of the fight was through the township within the hour. To most experts, I learned afterwards, it was a foregone walkover. To my own pal Ted it was a tragedy.

"I wouldn't mind you gettin' an ordinary pasting," he said. "You're gettin' a bit cocky anyhow. But this 'ere Stevens is a real bad egg."

"Perhaps I can be pretty bad, too," I retorted.

"You're so bad you're rotten," he snarled and went off in a hurry to see Ryan, the bruiser. Old Mick, so I was told much later by Ted, was anything but helpful.

"If Rogers the cop says the fight's on," Ryan told him, "you can bet your last zack it's on. That's the way our cop keeps the peace around here. Your pal will get half-killed. If I was you I'd warn the hospital and have me a stretcher down at the stockyard. No kiddin'. I only got to stroke Bluey with a sixteen-ounce glove and he gets so sick he scares me. He's going to get stoushed good and proper is your pal. Yip. Nasty little cove, that jockey feller.

"I seen him once drinkin' a pint alone in a pub across at Winton. Blokes who drink alone are no good, chum. And some shearer, bloke about fourteen stone, started up about some race Stevens lost. Stevens don't take no notice. The shearer goes on about this race is crooked. And suddenly the little jock sorter sprung at him. I think he musta bin wearing a ring with a sharp stone or somethink in it. You wanter watch that. He cut that shearer to ribbons. Put the feller in hospital fer three munce. He's wicked, is Stevens."

Ted listened with rising apprehension. "If Bluey gets it

that bad," he said, "I'll cut that swine's throat, s'elp me Jesus. I've gotter get it stopped. It's murder, that's what it is."

Old Mick made sympathetic grunts through his broken nose. "A fight's a fight, chum."

That was the inexorable fact. Eleven o'clock on a Sunday morning at the stockyard back of the railway station was a fixture for a declared fight as immutable as sunrise. Every Barcaldine male was there. Women were not allowed. A fight at the stockyard was a fair fight, properly refereed, with two-minute rounds signalled by the cop's whistle, fought according to Marquess of Queensberry rules so far as the referee honestly knew them, and the fight ended when one man or the other was completely and utterly beaten.

Rogers found it saved him a lot of work running in the rowdies and drunks for disturbing the peace, and the township regarded the arrangement as second only in entertainment value to the annual race meeting. Folk came in from the sheep stations forty and fifty miles around. Everyone put on a clean shirt. Publicans fixed sweepstakes on the number of rounds the fight would last. Hundreds of gallons of beer were swallowed before and after.

The fact that one contestant might be twice as big as the other had no significance except that the fun might be rather poor. It was a fight, and what it was all about was nobody's business.

Ted thought this was horribly like throwing Christians to the lions at a Roman circus. He made his views so clear with pointed Cockney epithets, that he would have found himself with several fights on his own hands if the broadminded citizens had not discounted heavily on his insults because he was from the Old Country and knew no better.

The argument happened on a Wednesday, and on Wednesday afternoon I went confidently into special training, under the tutelage of the middleweight champion of All Western Queensland. Special training included extra breathing exercises, extra skipping for fast footwork and earnest discussion on diet. Mick advised me to soak my hands in vinegar every night. "Mighty hard on the hands, this raw knuckle stuff," said the old campaigner with a grin. "Vinegar will toughen 'em, kiddo."

"You think I can lick him, Mick?" There might have been the faintest tinge of doubt in my voice. No more.

"Not a chance in a million," said Mick cheerfully.

I laughed but stumbled on the whirling skipping rope. After all, I was a head taller, probably much quicker and fitter and I had the old one-two.

"Not a chance in fifty million," said Mick. "If you ask me, you're goin' to get stoushed pretty bad. That feller Stevens is nasty. My oath."

"What do you want to talk that way for?" said Ted angrily. "Tryin' to frighten him out of the fight? Bluey's goin' to win, and you know it. Stevens," he sneered. "I'd spit in his eye meself, and I'm no fighter."

The pug was abashed by his Cockney vehemence. He understood vaguely that Ted was taking this line to boost my morale, but it didn't make sense to him.

I looked from one to the other, puzzled and uneasy.

"Mick was joking," said my pal. "Wasn't you?"

"Sure, I was joking, kiddo," said old Mick, mildly. "Still, you better get on with that skippin', and then you better get a couple of steaks inside you and go to bed early."

I followed instructions faithfully. I spent a couple of restless nights, picturing a hundred things happening at the stockyard. Generally, I saw myself winning a hero's battle against desperate odds. Sometimes I almost succumbed to the temptation of speculating whether, by any unforeseen happening, the fight would be stopped, or abandoned. The rains, for instance, or illness. I wondered, could men be as bad, as ruthless, as savage, as the villainous-looking Stevens was reputed to be?

The faithful Ted dogged my steps moodily all day, his black brows drawn close above his peering eyes. He was short-sighted, but his hearing was keen and his tongue quick. He was in an ugly temper.

Stevens was seldom seen. The rest of Barcaldine forgot the fight in the business of the week.

On Friday, Mick was in good spirits. "Kiddo," he said, "I thought it all out. I seen this Stevens fight. He ain't really much if you got some boxing."

"Or an 'ammer," barked Ted.

"Go on, Mick," I said eagerly. "What did you think out?"

The pug struck a boxing stance. "I remember," he said, "he comes in duckin' an' weavin', like this. Crouchin'. See? Now, you got reach, and when you see him come in crouchin', you go in too. Understand? If you stand still he clouts you, and then it's bad, my oath it is. But you don't stand still and you don't back away. You step in while he's in the crouch, and you uppercut with the old left, fast. All you got, bang in the face. That jerks his head back—and before he gets his guard up, over comes the old right cross. Get the idea?"

Even Ted was dimly interested.

We tried it out, the old pro and I, over and over again. It looked good.

Three men from the town approached as I was dressing. "Your kid ain't got a cat in hell's chance," said one of them to Mick.

"Oh, I don't know," said Mick cautiously. "What sort of odds are you layin', anyway?"

"Hundred to a fiver."

Mick scratched his half bald pate. "Sounds a good bet to me, Snowy. I'll take it twice."

"You're on," said the bookmaker. He wrote it in a little book. "Never take the judgment of a jockey or a fighter. They're our best customers."

"Oh, I don't know," said Mick. "This English kid's got somethin'."

"Where's he got it?" jeered the bookmaker, eyeing my lengthy frame.

"Well, I seen boxin' a good many years," said Mick thoughtfully, "and the way this kid's picked it up is just miraculous. Sort of Jimmy Wilde wallop. Maybe Stevens don't get younger, neither. I like my bet, Snowy."

"I hope you got the tenner," retorted the bookmaker as he left. His tone was just perceptibly less dogmatic.

"I hope you got the two hundred," said Mick softly.

Ted stared hard, his sharp eyes on Mick's. "Are you crazy?" he snapped at him.

"I jus' took a good bet," protested Mick. "The kid's come on a ton. You seen it yerself. Twenty to one? Never was such odds in any fight. I jus' took a good bet, pal. By tomorrow young Bluey 'll have that left uppercut perfect. Cripes! I oughter know, didn't I? I seen that Stevens. He ain't nothin' against a good left uppercut."

Ted was filled with dark suspicions, and he was the more bitter because he didn't know yet what he suspected. It didn't add up. Ten pounds was a heap of money to this broken-down bruiser.

"Somebody's making a bleeding fool of hisself," he said. "Either you or that bookie. But I ain't quite so stoopid, see?"

"The kid's improved, I tell yer," said Mick with some enthusiasm. "Most of youse newchums can't fight a damn, but now and again one comes up with everything. That's how it is with Bluey. Maybe he ain't a cert to win. But I give him a chance. Now I'm the best judge around the west, ain't I? I can lick anyone in the bush. I might of been a world champ if I'd gone to Sydney when they wanted me." He looked around and lowered his voice. "Take my tip. Rake up all your dough and take the odds on Bluey, because I think he's goin' to win."

Ted thrust out his jaw. "Now I'll tell you something," he snapped. "This fight is goin' to be stopped."

Mick's mouth opened as though he had been kicked in the stomach. I came in closer to hear what Ted was worrying about.

"You can't kid me," Ted sneered at him. "Wednesday you're tellin' us Bluey 'll be murdered and Friday you're sayin' the other feller's easy meat. This fight don't go on. I'm sending a wire to the chief commissioner of police at Brisbane. We'll see if Rogers can run this town as he pleases. The law don't allow people to be butchered because the local cop thinks he's Henry the Eighth."

He turned.

144

"Wait on," called Mick. "Look," he said, persuasively, "I think you're dead right to stand by yer pal. Dead right, see? My oath. He's a good kid, is Bluey. I like him, don' I? I wouldn't let this Stevens knock him to pieces. Why, I got a kid of me own. Maybe you didn't know that. Well, I have. Now, this fight on Sunday. You don't have to worry about it, it's practically in the bag."

Ted never took his eyes off the pug's broken face. "How d'you mean?"

Mick hesitated.

"When we say in England that it's in the bag," said Ted, measuring his words, "we mean it's fixed. Crook."

To Ted the situation was crystal clear, and as we went back through the dusty streets he realised that it was he, Ted, who was now on the spot. My thoughts were far away but Ted's were concentrated on his problem. The fight was to be a frame-up. Stevens and Ryan were cashing in. Ryan was teaching me to attack in a certain way and Stevens would take a dive. A couple of swings from me, and Stevens would fake a knock-out.

Stevens, through friends, had no doubt been backing me at long odds. The fake would deceive no one, for I had no experience at all, not even a natural punch. My name would stink. But Ryan and Stevens would collect. A bet was a bet, and both had something to back up their claims. Stevens was an ugly customer.

But Ted spoke none of these thoughts to me. I went to bed excited and almost happy. Stories were drifting around the bars that the skinny English lad was no fool at the fight game. Betting increased and the odds shortened, though still heavily favouring Stevens.

On the Saturday a crowd came over to the bath to see me in training, but Mick warned them off. "No bastard's going to see my man in action. Don't want no spies."

Stevens wasn't bothering to train. In fact he was drinking more heavily than usual.

Ted, the shrewd Cockney, now saw the whole scheme as plainly as if he had planned it himself. But he did not see the answer. Alone on Saturday night he set out the problem something like this: if he told me his suspicions I would undoubtedly blow up the whole thing. I would have no part in a frame-up—William Ewart Gladstone would have haunted me for the rest of my life. I'd rather have forced a straight fight and risked being half killed.

But, thought Ted, it would be horribly wrong to let me take part in ignorance in a crooked fight. Everyone would know it was crooked. The story would run from east to west and north to south of the Queensland outback. It would follow me wherever I went. Ted played with the idea of threatening Stevens with exposure, but realised that if he did, I would probably get the worst that Stevens could dish out. Which, from all accounts, was a form of torture and mutilation that Stevens had perfected for chumps like me.

I heard Ted turning restlessly and called to him: "You think I'm going to win, don't you Ted?"

"I hope you kill the bleeder," he said.

To my surprise and disappointment nobody took any particular notice of me next morning as I crossed the road and made my way past the line of hotels, through the station and on to the stockyard. Just when passing one pub I heard a chap say: "That's the kid that's fighting Stevens." The other said, "Oh, him." The fight mattered. Not the fighters.

When I arrived, with Ted and my chief second, Mick Ryan, just before eleven, the top rails of the stockyard were crowded with men and boys. Some said: "Good luck, Mick." "You see," said Mick, "they're all shoutin' for us. That's a good sign. The crowd genr'ally knows. Now let's go over them tactics agen."

The stockyard was a forty-yard square of churned sandy earth, smelling sickeningly of dung. I had a slight shock when I looked across at my opponent and realised his enormous physique when stripped. His broad shoulders and flexing neck muscles were flanked by long, heavy-boned arms. I took off my own shirt and felt naked as the tropical sun drove into my white midriff.

146

In that moment I knew that, although I was reasonably fit and strong and had shed entirely the frailness of earlier years, there was far too much small-boned length in my torso for this business of fighting. One needed heavy bones, as well as guts, to stand punishment.

Rogers the cop loosened his tunic-shirt, climbed through the lower rail and came across to my corner.

"Two-minute rounds. Fair fighting, Queensberry Rules, and stop when I tell you. Give you five minutes to get ready."

"What's Queensberry Rules?" I asked Mick.

"Don't bother with it," he said. "Simply says you shouldn't butt 'im nor kick 'im in the balls."

The cop was about to speak when Ted broke in. "You know the Marquess of Queensberry Rules?" he asked Rogers.

"I am the Marquess of Queensberry," said the cop, "around these parts."

"Well then," said Ted, "you know you have to stop the fight when one man can't win, to stop unnecessary punishment. You know that?"

The cop looked suspiciously to each of the three of us. "No bloody sauce," he said as he walked away.

"He jess feels sorry fer Stevens," Ryan called after him, and that cheered me up quite a bit, for the moment.

Mick gave me his last words. "Spar around a bit. Keep poking out the old left and wait till he rushes. Then give him the uppercut with all you've got. Don't forget, Bluey. *All you've got.*"

Ted also added some last words. "Only way to treat bleeders like Stevens, you gotter get stuck with everything, fair and foul, boots and bloody elbows. Never mind a cuss about the cop. Stevens is a rat, ole pal. Don' let 'm lay down. Cane the bastard once and fer all."

One hoarse " 'Luck, Bluey" from the rails reached me. The piano player, I guessed. No one else spoke at all. Stevens was no favourite with the mob. Me, I was nothing. It was a long lonely walk to the middle of the stockyard and I had plenty of time to shrug off the trembling sensation and clear my confused mind.

But in fact I could do neither. I simply realised suddenly that Stevens was facing me within punching distance and that this was it. I raised my guard and started to circle on my toes according to the book. Stevens looked me steadily in the eye as he moved half a step to my six. He looked at me just as a snake looks when challenging, a cold merciless destroyer.

Still no sound from the rails. I shot out my left and missed by two feet. I tried again and missed again. Stevens made no move. The silent pantomime went on for half the round, without a blow being landed, and then a voice from the rails broke through. "Get stuck in fer Gawdsake." I circled again, and a second voice shouted: "Taking a dive, Stevens?" And a third: "Which way you betting, Stevens?"

Stevens took his eyes off me, for the first time, and looked round to see who was baiting him, and in that second I hit him flush on the mouth and swung my right, in the follow up, into his ear. As I stepped away, feeling much better, he feinted and hit me a smashing blow on the nose.

It was the first man-size punch I'd ever received, apart from the fracas in the Brisbane pub, and for several long seconds I was virtually helpless, my eyes filled with water, blood streaming over my mouth and my lips swelling up. But Stevens fenced around until I was more or less in control of myself again.

Then he stamped his front foot, and this alerted me. Stevens had a habit of stamping before he attacked, Mick had said. In that split second I lowered my left arm, turning the knuckle in, as so often practised, and as Stevens came in with his crouch I caught him an uppercut somewhere on his face with all the force I could put under it, from my ankles upwards.

Stevens' head shot back and he staggered away, too far for me to reach him with the second part of the synchronised one-two, and this threw everything out of timing. Though I knew nothing of it, it also threw out of gear the plan in which Stevens was to take the dive. My second punch couldn't be delivered.

148

But I had an irresistible urge to do something, something big, something devastating, before Stevens could recover from the uppercut, and without science or skill to guide me I leapt at him as he reeled and thrashed at him with flailing fists.

Now Stevens was also fighting mad. He hit me three sickening punches, so that I was half-blinded, and brain-numbed. Blood was running down my chest—that I remember. But what I did from then on was done from sheer instinct, without any conscious direction or awareness, but just fighting savagery, like the two halves of a severed soldier ant fighting each other.

They told me I went into Stevens with everything—that I butted him and broke his nose, banged my knee into his groin and when he fell I crashed into him on the hard sandy floor, full weight knees first into his stomach.

Now the crowd were roaring, but of this I heard nothing, nor even Rogers' whistle in my ear. With Stevens underneath and badly hurt, I clutched his throat with both hands and banged his head against the ground. Stevens managed to hook me off him, but before he was fairly on his feet I jumped head-on into him again and the two of us were now rolling over in the hot dust.

The cop was a big brawny man, but tackling the writhing mass of trousers, heads and elbows was like grappling an octopus in a sandstorm. Eventually, so it was related to me, Rogers grabbed one dungareed leg firmly and hauled its owner away.

That was myself. I lay sobbing up great gusts of air, while Stevens crawled away on all fours, unable to stand up. Dimly, I observed that. It was almost the only part of the fight that I remembered afterwards.

In his best announcer voice the cop pronounced his verdict. Pointing to me as I lay on the sand he said: "You're disqualified under the Marquess of Queensberry Rules fer jumpin', swearin', buttin', hittin' below the belt, kickin' and fightin' on the mat. Get outer this township before sun-up tomorrow."

Pointing to Stevens he added: "You get out before sun-down ternight. And don't come back."

This started a hullaballoo. "Stevens musta won, ref," shouted a bookie. "You disqualified the English feller."

Rogers, the oracle, had the answer. "Both disqualified. Stevens never tried a yard."

"What about the bets, Rogers?" yelled the boys on the rails.

"All bets off," said Rogers, "No contest."

I imagine the menfolk of Barcaldine agreed, as they made for the pubs, that Rogers had done a good job. The purity of the stockyard had been sullied. Or was I wrong?

Ryan had disappeared. Ted and the piano-player helped me to my corner, sloshed the bucket of water over my bleeding head, and half carried me across to the pub.

"You done well," Ted was saying over and over again. "You done real well, pal."

They put me in a room to myself. I was barely conscious an hour later, trying to swallow some neat whisky which made me sick, while someone held an ice-pack over my face.

A smartly dressed bush type came in at one stage, looked searchingly at me, and said: "I heard Rogers tell you to get out of town tomorrow."

"We leave when we decide," growled Ted. "A cop ain't the law. Who are you?"

Without any change of inflection the stranger said, "If you two want work I can use you out at the Downs for a few weeks. Lamb-marking. Thirty bob and tucker."

I was beyond speech. The sense of things happening around me was just filtering through as I heard Ted tell him we'd be glad to take it but his pal would need a couple of days' rest. Sure, said the stranger, he'd fix it with Rogers and the station buggy would be along Wednesday after breakfast.

CHAPTER SIXTEEN
Lonely? I got me dawg

IF THE Marquess of Queensberry's Rules had been kicked around in the stockyard dung, the tattered cause of Old Country immigrants seemed to have been given a sharp uplift. Myself, I spent two days in bed.

I was in a messy state. Both eyes were blackened and all but closed by swellings, the whole of my mouth and nose was merged into a puffed heap too tender for the lightest touch and a bang on one ear had left an appalling ache. A deep cut was covered with plaster.

Someone came and examined me, covered my face with ointment and strapped up my left hand and wrist—my knuckles were bruised and torn open and a bone was dislocated somewhere. I was fed at times by the barmaid with the Midlands accent and when she came in I could recognise her perfume but couldn't see her. I had liked her as a very cheery sort.

A drunk found his way to my room while Ted was absent eating his dinner. He set two pints of beer beside me and said: "G'luck, chum. Bes' leftook I ever seen." He then sank both pints without drawing breath and staggered out.

When I could speak I said to Ted: "I can't understand that first punch. It must have been that I was in such a panic that I lashed out with my eyes shut, moving in like Mick told me, and he sort of fell on it. I thought I'd broken my arm."

"Well," said Ted. He grinned. "I seen some rough houses, back home outside the pubs of a Sunday night closing time, but I never seen nothing as foul as you was. It was the filthiest ever. Stevens 'ad to be lifted onto his 'orse last night. They said he wouldn't be no good to a woman fer a bit."

"You mean . . .?"

"The second fall, when you jumped him feet first."

"I don't remember that. I don't remember anything after he bashed me. Not a thing."

"They're still talking about it in the pubs," he said complacently. "Blokes drop in downstairs to ask how you are. 'Course, that fathead pianist says he could make you a champion with that left hook . . ."

"But I haven't got a left hook, Ted. I haven't got anything."

"I know, kiddo," he soothed. "You ain't got no boxing. But you got guts. I never would of thought it. You got guts, and that's what matters to these people."

I had no reply to that because after the bashing I had received I had no idea how I would act if put to the test again. "It's what Mick said, I suppose. You've got to be ready and willing to fight, even if you never have to. But they have to know it."

"They know it, Bluey, old sport. That feller who offered us a job is the son of a big squatter somewhere around. He seen the fight. I s'pose it was his way of sorter saying you done well."

"My God, what a way to get a job!"

"Still, we got a job, boyo. I didn't tell you before but a bloke called Mr Bannister also blew in. Appears he's a shearing contractor—got a connection around the smaller selectors. Said we could have a job with him any time. Ain't that good?"

It made me feel fine. On the Tuesday I sauntered over to the swimming bath, still battle-scarred. "Hi, Bluey" was the greeting from folk who had never noticed me before.

Mick was winding up his training. " 'Sright," he said. "Always takes coupla days to get over a good fight. Bluey, you gave him the uppercut good-oh, but you lost control. You lost me two hundred quid, too," he added ruefully.

"You'd only 'ave boozed the lot," said the candid Ted.

"Maybe," the old prizefighter grunted as he shadow punched. "But what a booze-up. Now I have to knock out this Clermont stiff fer ten lousy quid. What a purse fer defendin' my title!"

"How do you see it, Micko?" I asked him, almost professionally.

He winked. "This one's in the bag, too, but the other feller don't know it yet."

Late that night I escaped from the bar of our pub, to the disappointment of the publican, and went to bed to write home. I told the old folk I was about to go on an important job lamb-marking but couldn't say yet whether there was any future in it. At two in the morning I heard the publican shut the front door and lock up.

A little later my bedroom door opened softly—my light was still on—and Annie, the barmaid, came in, put a bottle of Johnnie Walker and two glasses silently on the side table, signalled to me to be quiet (the room divisions were of thin wood) and closed the door. She was in her dressing gown, with her long flaxen hair brushed down to her waist. She was a well-made thirty or so. It was a hot night and the last thing I wanted was whisky raw.

She poured two noggins, whispered, "Hot, 'nt it?" as she pushed her dressing gown off her plump shoulders, revealing the first pair of women's breasts I had seen at close quarters, and whispered: "I'm from the Old Dart, too. Came over with my family when I was three. We got to stick together, Bluey, don't we? Bungo."

"Bungo," I said and swallowed some Johnnie Walker.

She then put out the light and I heard her say: "Shove over a bit, me dear."

So Annie was the first woman I bedded. Victor's spoils, quite in Roman style. It was a hot, perspiratory affair, rendered possible only by the patience and skill of Annie. An hour later she kissed me on the most painful part of my mouth, slipped out of bed, took both glasses and the bottle and disappeared without a sound.

I felt neither shocked nor excited—just pleased and perhaps exultant. "Holy poker," I muttered to myself, "now I know what it's all about. I'm glad it happened just like that." William Ewart Gladstone wasn't in this race.

Next morning came the buggy from the Downs, a sheep station some thirty miles out, of average size for the west at that time with fifty to sixty thousand head of sheep, mostly merino ewes and hoggets. Ted and I rolled our swags once more, left our sundowner trappings with our landlord and were driven out of Barcaldine in style. I found a cigar someone had given me, realised I couldn't smoke it, wouldn't be able to smoke anything for a while, and handed it to the astonished driver.

The boss's son, Dick, met us as we climbed down in the homestead paddock.

"Thanks for the job," I said.

"I saw the fight," he said. "They told me it was going to be crook! That jockey feller, Stevens. He must have done something pretty raw to make you so mad."

Strange. It hadn't occurred to me. "It was over some kid's bike pump," I said.

He stared at me for a moment. "Well, blind old Riley. I wouldn't have thought it. You must be a real son of a bitch when someone upsets your beer."

He took us over to the station hands' quarters.

"You'd better eat here before you join the team. Last decent feed for two or three weeks. I've told the cook to lay on some corned beef—it'll be all mutton till you finish the marking."

"Only two or three weeks' work?" asked Ted.

"We'll see," was the noncommittal reply. "Just thought we'd help out. Must be hard going for you blokes till you settle in out here."

We joined the team by a distant creek just before dusk and dumped our swags in a vacant tent. The set-up was similar to my first job, in New South Wales (how many many years ago), same sunburnt, ageless bush types, cook with a short temper always on the verge of asking for his time, a jackeroo type overseer, a head man, and some permanent station hands with their horses.

Joining up was no longer an ordeal. We still doubtless bore the marks of the immigrant but at least we were dressed and equipped for the bush, knew the authentic language of the bush in all its participles and implications, and observed the camp fire ritual.

154

They all knew about the fight. The cook gave me the biggest plateful of roast meat I'd ever faced. Someone offered me a cigarette and we were invited into a game of crib. I could play a pretty shrewd hand. Cribbage, I had found, was even more a demand on one's capacity for mental arithmetic than most other card games. Playing a good game of crib gave one status in the bush.

At dawn we had a pannikin of scalding tea and a cake and went over to the scene of operations for an hour or so of work before breakfast. Where two paddocks joined, a mob of ewes with their lambs was being eased slowly by the riders and their dogs into the corner of the paddock. Here, a gate was opened into the other paddock, and as the ewes jumped over an imaginary obstacle through the gate opening, the lambs were steered away into a pen.

Now we had some five hundred lambs huddled in the pen, bleating pathetically, while outside, calling back in a frantic medley as they wandered aimlessly back and forth, were the mothers. The air was thick with dust and the familiar stink of unscoured wool hung around one.

Following the lead of others inside the pen, I grabbed a lamb and sat it on the top rail. It was no more than a week old, a tiny thing with a piping voice. It happened to be a ewe lamb. First to pass along the line of lambs sitting on the fence was the chap with the branding clippers, who clipped a piece neatly out of the lamb's left ear. I felt this must be unnecessarily barbaric.

The clipper was followed by the chopper, who grabbed the lamb's tail and with a short blow severed it. The lamb reacted with a spasm, but relapsed dejectedly. I put it down outside the fence as gently as I could, and it doddled off searching and calling among the mob of ewes.

My next lamb was bigger and stronger. He took some holding on the fence. After his ear was clipped and his tail docked came the ganger. Dressed in a butcher's blue apron, his hands, face and apron were bloody and quite appalling to the unaccustomed eye. He took the struggling young lamb's purse and slit the end off with his knife. And then, dropping the knife, he pressed his two thumbs into the lamb's groins and with his teeth extracted the protruding testicles and spat them out. The young ram was now a hogget.

I managed no more than a dozen lambs before feeling obliged to say to the ganger "Taken short" and walked hastily to a nearby clump of mulga scrub where I vomited. When I came back the ganger said: "You musta taken a packet last Sunday, Bluey. Take it easy. Back to camp and start again after breakfast."

I looked around. There was Ted, stolidly grabbing his lambs and cursing the stragglers in good old Saxon. "I'll be all right," I said, and I was, just. The breakfast was a bit trying. But sensitiveness to this sort of thing never lasted very long, in a job that had to be repeated over and over again.

I never ceased to speculate as I watched the newly marked lambs hobbling into the great dust cloud where ewes and lambs wandered round and around in their search, what percentage of lambs ever found their own mothers. It didn't appear to be important. A ewe would have three or four lambs at her teats, probably none of her own offspring.

Overhead the sparrowhawks circled and higher still the great carrion birds waited, while the crows hopped around as close as they dared. All were looking for victims, but the most cowardly and cruel of these was the crow, the enemy of every other land creature. The crow would never tackle its victim, however harmless or small, until it was quite helpless, and then its methods of feeding were diabolical. No doubt the crows fitted in somewhere in nature's pattern of the life cycle, but I never lost the desire to shoot them.

After a few days we cleaned up the mobs in this part of the vast station and rode fifteen or twenty miles to the next camp. Here we found the station team already mustering, and we set about fixing the pen and making a camp. The grub on this job was better than anything I'd ever had in the bush—spuds, even onions for the cook to make a stew as a change, good bread, bacon for breakfast on Sundays, and of course mutton for the rest. The ganger gave me a horse to ride between camps, which in some way indicated that he regarded me as something special. "I only hope," I confided to Ted, "he doesn't offer to let me try his job. I'd go right down to the bottom of his list at once."

All this special treatment was very welcome, though I felt I was a mountebank. "Considering I put up such a stinking fight," I said to Ted one Sunday, "and got myself disqualified and banished from the town, and especially as I'm English and the chap I jumped on was Australian, I'd have thought people would have kicked me out of the state."

Ted drew deeply on his cigarette. "Yet I woulda felt the same as they do if I hadn't even known you. Two reasons, I think. One, *because* you're an immigrant and still only halfgrown, and the other, because it looked a dead cert you'd be cut to pieces. The Australians love to see the underdog win. Didn't their forefathers all be gaolbirds exported from the Old Country in chain gangs or something?"

We finished the gory business in three or four weeks, and I thought Dick, the boss's son, looked pleased to see me ride into the home paddock, take off the saddle and bridle, and give my mount the customary spank on the behind which means "Thanks, pal."

"You want to stay on a bit?" he asked, after we'd eaten. "I could give Bluey another three weeks, as he can manage a horse. What about you, Ted?"

"You got anything mechanical?" said Ted. "Anything from an electric tramcar to a kid's toy truck, and I kin fix it."

"You're my man," was the immediate response. "We've got a new electric plant here for the house which no one understands, and it's always going wrong."

So for three weeks Ted fiddled with the dynamo or whatever it was, and I rode off with an old hand who looked like eighty and rode like eighteen, and Jackie the Aboriginal. We took some grub and a gun and set out on a tour of the boundary fences, waterholes, dams, bore drains and all the odd places where a sheep can get itself trapped and must await slow death under the burning sun, watched by the crows. Here and there we came on a lone boundary rider, living with his horse and his dog in a remote hut, visited once a month by the ration cart, with a month every year back in civilisation.

After surviving chafed thighs, I found the journey exciting. During my swag humping the bush looked the same monotonous plain every day from dawn till sunset, but riding the fences brought new scenes, new experiences. Once I had watched Jackie cut the throat of a young sheep, or break the neck of a jack rabbit, I could get interested in the art of skinning and cutting and the messy cleaning business. Jackie could look at a waterhole for a full minute and say: "Fish. Me catchum." He could perform many mysteries, and if the truth were admitted, he was probably worth more to the station owners than three white men.

We mended fences broken by kangaroos or emus, marked rabbit burrows for destruction later, set traps for dingoes, saved lost lambs from the menacing crows, exchanged tobacco with the boundary riders, shot and buried a sheep dying of cancer, and came back to report that all was well with the hundreds of miles of the Downs and its sixty thousand inhabitants.

I had a crack with a grizzled old boundary rider one night when we camped at his hut. I couldn't understand how a man could bear the loneliness of his life. He poked the logs into a blaze, deep in thought, and eventually came out with: "It's what a man get useter, shouldn't y' think?"

"But with no one to talk to, even?"

"Oh. Yair. Well, I got me dawg. I talk a lot to me dawg." Then his reflective drawl changed to something sharper. "An' them bastard crows. I talk to them, the bastards. They're always there, settin' on the fence, starin' at me. They sorter hope I'm goin' ter die. Them bastard crows, always waitin' fer something to start to die. I often seen a crowd of 'em set on a tiny lamb deserted by its mother and scarce old enough to walk. Pecking the poor little devil to bits, eating it alive. They squark at me and me dawg when we come up with them like we didn' have no rights to interfere with 'em. Bastards."

"You shoot 'em?"

He shook his head. "Useter. Waste of good cartridges. Jess now and again I shoot a big one, the boss of the crowd and hang his carcase to rot on the fence over there, and I say to his mates: There's yer breakfast, yer bastards. Eat yer grandpa!"

"Do they?"

"Crows is carrion and their flesh is black. Only ants and flies eat a dead crow."

His dog lay a couple of yards away, never closer unless he called, never making an approach, friendly or otherwise, to us, the visitors. The little sheep dog was forever a one-man dog, his servant, his guardian and his brilliantly intelligent assistant.

CHAPTER SEVENTEEN

The fair dinkum world's record

WE CAME BACK into Barcaldine to find Billy the piano player in the bar, asking about us. "You're just the blokes I want, just in time," he said. "You heard about it all, no doubt?"

"Billy," said Ted, kindly, "we bin out in the blue seven weeks. I'm going to get me a bath and a feed of steak, beef steak, with three eggs on top and two pints of what they call beer."

"Me too," I agreed.

But nothing could stop Billy, to whom his piano playing was more important than the escape of Pearl White in the serial. What he had to say now was more important than our hunger and thirst combined.

"I got the posters all over the town. Prob'ly all Australia has heard about it, and people will be waiting up all night for the news right across as far as Perth. It's the biggest thing the west has ever seen, boys, and you two lads are going to be right in it with us."

"This the skating thing?" Ted called from the shower.

Billy talked so fast I hardly got more than the drift of it before he was gone, shouting back over his shouders: "See you at the rink in an hour. If you can't get in, ask fer me."

Billy was certainly looking every inch the promoter of a world shattering event when he paid our zacks and entered the crowded skating rink. He switched on the lights, raised his home-made megaphone majestically and announced: "Everybody off the rink, please." As one man they all pulled into the sides.

"Quiet, please. Now Pete Martin, champion Australian roller skater, will give a special exhibition of high speed skating. This is part of his training for his world championship record skate at this rink starting on Friday next!"

Billy had had a piano brought to the rink, and as our handsome Pete flashed around the rink, fast and faster, Billy rattled out the piece he reserved in the cinema for charging Indians and the chase of the stage coach. Billy led the applause as Pete finished with a dozen spectacular leaps and spins.

"Pete," announced Billy, "will now resume his training for his world championship skate, starting next Friday, when Pete will attempt to set up a new world's skating endurance record *for one hundred hours*. Non-stop, friends. Right here on this rink in Barcaldine. And you can all help Pete and share in the honour and glory of this marvellous Australian triumph. If he succeeds he will owe everything to all you folk.

"So help him by being here every day when he trains, and when the Great Skate starts, come in as often as you can, day and night, and keep him company. And then you, my friends, will be able to say with pride: I skated with Pete Martin, right alongside, when he was making his wonderful, his all-time, world's non-stop, world's record skate of one hundred hours on the rink at Barcaldine!"

Tremendous applause greeted this speech and when Pete bowed Billy bowed too.

With the session concluded, Billy checked the sixpences with the owner of the rink and we four crossed the street to the Queen's.

"Well, boys?"

"Amazin'. Simply amazin'," said Ted. "All them people paying real money. I mean, how d'you work it out, people being all that interested in how long a feller can skate? Because what does it matter?"

Ted was really anxious not to be rude and making a rotten job of it, but Billy brushed it all aside.

"You bushwhackers," he said—and what a compliment, though he couldn't be expected to realise it—"you bushwhackers never see a newspaper and don't know what goes on the other side of the creek. Everyone's crazy about endurance records. Everyone, all over the world today.

"When I was in Melb'ne two years ago a feller stood on the stage of the Bijou Theatre and swung Indian clubs for three days and nights without stopping, and the theatre was filling up all the while with people paying their shills to see him. Three days and nights—only seventy-two hours and all he's got to do is stand there and swing them clubs, which is a kid's idea of fun any day.

"Well, that feller had a stage tour afterwards and even went to Europe. He was billed everywhere as the world's champion Indian club world record holder. Then there were the skipping people. And a bloke in Japan or somewhere spun a diabolo for forty-eight hours. Why? The dough, pal, the dough!

"And another bloke nearly killed himself when he fell asleep trying to beat the endurance record standing on stilts. It's all sensational, don't you see? They all come to look at him, like he was some weird animal outer the bush. And how does he manage, the women ask, about his bowels and all that."

"That's a point," I put in here. "How does he manage?"

Billy ignored the question as not worth answering. "The record endurance for roller skating," he went on with his spiel, "is eighty-four hours, by some Greek or Italian somewhere. We're not just going to beat it. We're going to knock it to smithereens. We're going to skate for one hundred bloody hours. Think of the publicity! The newspapers! Photographs! We'll get offers to come and show ourselves from all over the world."

Billy's publicity—considering that Barcaldine had no newspaper except the one that came up from Rockhampton two or three times a week, and that radio was not yet born —showed that Billy was ahead of his day. He used the cinema screen for hand-drawn announcements which he wrote himself, had little posters fixed for nothing on the store counters and in the saloon bars—and one in the police house—and had wheedled mail riders to take handbills out to the sheep stations on their weekly rounds.

He arranged a team of honorary referees, from whom a

162

rota was drawn so that at least one member was on duty throughout, day and night, to sign a large sheet after every session, pasted up for all to see, certifying that Pete had skated continuously and without help.

"This one is straight up," said Billy. "No Greek nor no Italian concerned in this lark. It's fair dinkum all the way."

"Square an' all," I added.

Billy had fixed the skate to start at three o'clock on a Friday afternoon. He calculated that if Pete was still alive and skating at three o'clock on Tuesday, the last four dramatic hours would arouse a crescendo of excitement culminating in a terrific scene from the rink packed with every citizen of Barcaldine who could raise the shill to get in.

We had a letter from Hugh. "The job didn't pan out too good . . . Yes, we washed out some sapphire, not very good quality but enough to pay for tucker and a bit over . . . terrible work, digging out heavy soil down a shaft by flares, hotter than hell, no air to breathe . . . always hoping to strike a patch and be rich, but the other chaps had been hoping like that for fifteen years. We packed up and left when the other chaps went on the shikker for a whole week and left us with no tucker. Now in Rocky and leaving here Tuesday by the express and should be in Barcaldine Thursday morning . . ."

"I'll be glad to see them," I said. "Pity they're not here for the big skate. I reckon those two can both skate pretty good."

Ted admitted he'd not be sorry to see them. "Though, mind you, we'll never rely on 'em again."

I felt the same way. We were now four friends but also two pairs of pals—no longer four straying immigrants huddled together like sheep for whatever protection there might be in numbers. Now, there were moments when I even wondered when the time would come for me to say to Ted, as the others had said to us, that I had a chance I must take alone, sorry and all that, pal. Ted, for his part, had performed wonders with that dynamo out at the Downs,

163

and his future might well lie along a path quite different from mine as we settled, if ever we did, into some permanent course in Australia.

The Great Skate was duly launched by a man generally regarded as Barcaldine's most important citizen, chairman of everything including even the annual race meeting committee and the magistrates. The whole panel of referees were there lined up, a fine body of men, some even wearing coats over their shirts, cheered by all the inhabitants that could squeeze into the rink.

Billy was at his greatest on his megaphone (I began to wonder if he slept with that thing). Pete looked trim, lean and handsome in his very special all-white rig and there was a dramatic hush as the most important man in Barcaldine stood with his watch while the seconds ticked away, and dead on three o'clock fired the starting pistol. Amid an explosion of cheering Pete was off.

For a dozen laps Barcaldine watched and admired, and then, having done its duty and had its thrill, left the rink and made for the pubs. Well, you had to drink in that bone-dry bush heat above Capricorn, whether it was hot tea or cold beer. "Otherwise," it was often pointed out to me, "a feller'd dry up like a dead tree."

As the hours crept along the severity of our hero's task became more and more obvious. At first all was well. Pete went on blithely through midnight into the small hours, when he decided to empty his bowels. We had to waken Billy to take charge of this operation, and to shake the dozing referee to witness that it was all performed according to Cocker.

Feeding Pete by skating alongside was comparatively simple, whereas holding a pan under him as he crouched along was tricky, and on the corners, impossible. Billy slithered on his backside several times before Pete was satisfied and pulled up his trousers. However, the chief thing, said Billy, was that it was all according to plan. Between two and three in the morning, Billy had told Pete, and Pete had duly come good.

164

"What about daytime, when spectators are around?" asked Ted.

"He'll have to wait," said Billy.

A small crowd turned up around six and seven in the morning to watch our champ shave and wash and eat his breakfast as he glided round the rink. Then Pete beckoned and whispered that he couldn't wait. Billy got his megaphone and announced, "All ladies out of the rink, please, for ten minutes."

They were back in time to see Pete being sluiced from a hose, and it seemed to me they felt important when they were asked to leave the rink.

All manner of people took keen delight in skating alongside to ask him "How're y' goin'?" and being told "Fine, pal, fine." Pete waltzed with the girls, did a bit of figure stuff and with one thing and another put up a show.

So the second night passed. Pete by now was looking a bit peaky and pale in the morning and his smile had become a bit mechanical. Now it was Sunday and a very hot day. The heat played hell with Pete, and Billy had his work cut out to maintain some colour in the performance. Pete had begun to lose interest in eating and wanted to drink large quantities of liquid so frequently that Billy had to apologise every time he had to say: "Ladies out of the rink, please. Sorry—can't be helped." Which made people feel uneasy.

During the day Pete began to get attacks of cramp and required much massaging. But just when he seemed to be arriving at a critical ebb his magnificent stamina enabled him to take fresh grip, and with spasmodic bursts of fancy skating and an occasional speed dash he forced his muscles back into the routine.

On Monday night Pete fell asleep. Fortune was with us. The rink was empty of visitors and the referee was also asleep. We were able to catch our man before he fell. A bucket of cold water revived him, Billy gave him a pill, and he staggered to his feet and went on.

"The pill," said Billy, "is quite harmless but the taste is so filthy it's guaranteed to keep him awake for an hour." But Pete fell asleep three times before the dawn came.

"I think he's about through," I said. "It'll do him no good to go on."

Billy wouldn't hear of it. "You don't know our Pete. If I let him stop now he'd murder me. We got to keep him going till daylight if we have to stick pins in him."

With the coming of dawn and the first shaft of warmth Billy woke me. I felt practically dead from fatigue, though I had dozed on and off throughout the skate on a bunk at the rink, and together we drenched our unhappy and almost unconscious hero with ice-cold water. Through the morning the crowds helped us to keep Pete awake and moving. He was skating with his eyes closed, and there were murmurs from some of the women about stopping the skate.

But the hour of triumph was approaching and the crowds, who had dwindled, began to flock in again.

"All these shills," said Billy, "don't mean a thing. The real dough comes later when we sign the big contracks and go on tour, Sydney, Melb'ne, London—who knows? He'll be world's champion. Jest think, boys, world's champ!"

Billy had to pull out every trick during the last few hours to prevent our man from falling. "Once he falls," Billy warned, "he'll never get up. Anyway, if he falls, or if anyone helps him, that's the official end of the skate. He's jest got to do it all alone."

So we worked on him, with massage, pills, pinching, keeping a gramophone record grinding out, and with cold douches. The poor chap moved along now with eyes closed, jaw sagging, face shrunken and grey. He made no response when spoken to. It seemed he was now moving in a mental vacuum, practically unconscious.

"Pete looks he's gonna drop dead," said one of the referees. "I think I'll call a meeting about him."

"Good idea," said Billy. "I'll call it for seven o'clock tonight."

But whether or not they thought it an inhuman task, the Barcaldine folk, who packed the rink at three o'clock, let out a most almighty burst of cheering when Billy announced that Pete had not only smashed the world's endurance record but had also skated four days and four nights which was ninety-six hours.

The noise awakened Pete from his comatose state. "Is it finished?" he muttered.

Billy gave him the merest sip of brandy. "Nearly there, pal. Nearly there. Nearly at the hundred hours." He took up his megaphone. "Give him all you've got, friends," he shouted. "Keep the lad going! *This is the greatest day of your lives!*"

Curious that my mind should go back to something similar said—according to Shakespeare—by Henry the Fifth. It occurred to me, too, that Billy's delivery was quite, quite different. But the result was the same, for the Barcaldine folk, like those English soldiers, responded magnificently, quite apart (as Billy said privately) from paying their dinars for the privilege. He banged the piano, though nearly dead himself, and Ted sang some rattling Cockney choruses.

So, amid the din, Pete survived crisis after crisis, until the most important man in Barcaldine strode into the middle of the rink, watch in hand, and eventually raised his arm and fired the starting pistol. It was seven o'clock. Men shouted, women burst into tears, Billy played "God Save the King" at his loudest, and Pete slid, graceful to the end, into a heap at the feet of the most important man.

As he lay there, out to the world, the committee of referees filed past, and each man bent down and shook Pete's limp right hand. And after we had carried Pete into the pay hut the rink slowly emptied and the pubs filled up once more. Thus the great Barcaldine Epic was seen to be accomplished and normality had been restored.

AT SEVEN O'CLOCK on the Thursday morning Hugh and Jack Hart walked into our pub as Annie was sweeping the bar with blouse unbuttoned. They came to our room and pulled back the mosquito netting.

Through sleepy eyes we looked up at them, Despite their fancy town suits they looked older and leaner.

"We bin skatin' for an 'undred hours," said Ted. "Bit wearin'!"

167

Jack said, "Ah. I read something about it in the Rockhampton paper. Last Tuesday, wasn't it?"

"Couldn't 'ave been in Tuesday's paper," Ted pointed out. "It didn't happen till Tuesday night."

"Well, that's strange." He went to his own room and came back with the paper, and searched it page by page and column by column. "Ah, here it is." He folded the paper and read the news brief. " 'Skate champ breaks his own record. Johann Schultz, holder of world's endurance roller skating record, completed a new skate record here tonight . . .' "

"Schultz? That's not us. Our man is Pete Martin!"

"Well, this says Johann Schultz. Maybe they've got the name wrong. 'Completed a new skate record here tonight of one hundred and twenty-eight hours!' "

"What!"

"Ah. I see. At the end of the message it says 'Associated Press, San Francisco.' So it's some other chap the other side of the world."

But nothing upset Billy for long, unless it was a prospect of real work. After a few days drowning his chagrin he blew into our joint to tell us that when the picture house closed for painting shortly he was going down to Rockhampton to play the piano in the window of a music shop for one hundred hours non-stop. Pete was to be Billy's trainer.

"This is something," said Billy, "that no Greek bastard in San Francisco can touch. This record will stand for all time."

CHAPTER EIGHTEEN

The Rev. Hulton Sams— boxing champ

"TIME WE GOT OUT of Barcaldine," said Ted at three o'clock one morning, as we turned in. "Time we got some work before me and Bluey become a couple of professional card sharps and Jack turns professional at two-up. Them shearers at the Royal said shearin' starts at Aramac in a week from now. First there gets the jobs."

It was forty miles north to Aramac, straight out into bush country. No more railway. Just bush track scarred by the hooves of the big wool teams. There was one pub, the "Halfway", which was just halfway between the town and Aramac. Many others were travelling the same track, shearers with their saddle and pack horses, three or four bumping along on motor cycles, an occasional buggy with some manager or other, cooks, engineers, and the lowest class of bush humanity bar the non-working sundowner, namely, the unskilled labourers, including ourselves, humping it out to look for jobs as rouseabouts on the shearing shed floor.

The pay for the rouseabout was a shilling an hour, but with tucker and shelter thrown in. A shed could last from four to six weeks. There was a wet-or-fine clause for us rouseabouts which was all-important, so we were told by the old hands along the track. Shearers can't shear wet sheep, and few sheds could pen up enough sheep to last more than a few hours. A good rain in Queensland could last a fortnight.

To the shearers, the woolclassers and a few others who worked piecework, rain could be a dead loss of time, but to the rouseabout the rain clouds were a signal for lifting hearts and the first few drops aroused cheers and shouts of "Send it down, Hughie!" A good rain meant a long lay-

169

off on full pay, with nothing to do but eat, play cards or read books from the shed library. Once shearing started, with the teams of men assembled and signed on, and the great droves of sheep on the move from various points, the job must be finished no matter how long the delays.

We took two days to reach the "Halfway", where Ted sang to the boys and a twenty-horse wagoner gave us a lift to Aramac as a token of a slight change of view of immigrants. We all got jobs, signed contracts and selected our bunks in a big unlined galvanised iron hut.

With winter approaching the temperature fell below zero at nights and so did I, shivering inside my one thin blanket with everything that might help piled on top. But by breakfast time it would be too hot to work in anything more than trousers and boots. Yet I never saw anyone with a cold all the time I was in the bush.

When the shear started the scene was as busily methodical as an antheap. The first mob of sheep was driven into the centre space of the shed and around the outer boundary of the shed, some three yards apart, were the shearers, with their mechanically driven, horse-clipper style shears. Behind the shearer was his small "in"-pen, kept filled from the centre space, and facing the shearer was a small chute leading to the "out"-pen, down which the bemused animal, sore but glad to be relieved of its heavy coat, was thrust to join the other naked-looking shornies.

Jack talked his way into the mustering squad and picked himself a high-spirited colt. Hugh bundled massively into the penning-up job. Ted was in charge of a section of the floor, his job being to gather each fleece, bring it to the wool rolling table, and throw it adroitly so that it spread like a rug, without breaking.

He was also in charge of the tar pot. This was a pot of creosote fluid, handed to the shearer as a sheep was finished, for creosote to be dabbed if necessary on the cuts the sheep had suffered during the three to four minutes of this high-speed shaving operation.

My job was at the wool table. I was shown how to trim off the soiled belly wool and the dags, which went into one bin, the flank wool into another bin, and then to roll what was left, the fine long-stapled shoulders and back into a self-tied bundle and pass it to his greatness, the man of mysterious knowledge, the classer.

The classer took a staple with the finicky neatness of a snufftaker, examined it, and ordered his assistant to place the fleece in one of his five or six bins, according to quality and type. How he performed his "classing" I never discovered, either from him or any other woolclasser. The classer was always ranked as a person of the highest skill and integrity, like a High Court judge, and was paid by the hundred, and very highly, they said. Woolclassing was an art supposed to be beyond the ken of ordinary bush folk.

Even the squatter himself, who quite possibly could be a millionaire if he ever bothered to sit down and work it out, regarded his classer with the sort of respect reserved for archbishops and champion jockeys.

The men upon whom the economic success of the shear depended were the shearers. The quicker the job was done, the cheaper the whole operation, and with wool fetching from sixpence ha'penny to tenpence a pound in Bradford, the cost of the clip was the biggest item against the profit margin, always excepting the droughts.

I had seen some hot jobs and some heavy jobs in Queensland, starting with the railway sleeper work at Mitchell with the sun blazing down on the metal at 130 degrees; then with fencing on rock on the Cunnamulla extension; the all-day-and-half-the-night of contract cane-cutting in the sweaty heat of the coast, and the wood-firing of the sugar mill. The power and stamina of the Australian always looked in my eyes to be manual labour raised to the nth degree in the world of work, and his pride in his output was amply justified and natural.

Now, in its own way, with its exceptional and unusual strains, I saw no job that equalled the demand on bodily aches, and the power to sustain them, of that of the shearer.

The day's scheduled eight hours and forty minutes had to be split into six periods of work. At five-thirty in the morning we helped ourselves to the tea, coffee and cakes laid out, and the first working spell was the longest of the day, from six till eight. The after-breakfast-until-dinner stretch was broken into two periods of eighty minutes, with a twenty-minute smoko, and the afternoon was split into three periods of eighty minutes with two smokos at the breaks. We finished at six in the evening and thus took twelve hours to fit in our eight hours forty minutes.

To me, with my long, slender back, the skill and ease with which the shearer worked at a heavy yet highly skilled job without once straightening his back throughout each entire period was a miracle of endurance. Bent double, he pulled the big, struggling sheep out of the pen as though it was a teddy bear and sat it on its haunches against his knees. The machine clipper was steered through the yellow pizzle wool and then, turning the sheep inside his knee, the shearer drove the machine so that it clove next to the skin from belly to throat, opening up the foamy, two-inch-long white coat like a knife piercing a wool mattress.

Steadily the machine pushed the coat off the neck, shoulders and sides, the sheep pivoting on its backside, until the whole fleece fell off in one piece, and the sheep sat there, white, bony and cool. A few daubs of stinging creosote where the blades had cut too deep, and the job was done.

Without straightening his back, the shearer took a few steps forward, lugging the sheep with him, shoved it down the "out" chute into daylight, turned back and grabbed the next one by a leg. Meanwhile, the fleece was removed from the floor by the rouseabout. The whole operation took between three and four minutes.

The shearers averaged 150 to 180 sheep a day, the younger men battling to do their hundred and the three-star men often topping the two hundred mark. Chief topic of talk during the run of every shed was always the tally shorn day by day. It was achievement that men were interested in, rather than the size of their cheques.

They were a tough but intelligent type, and despite the strain on the back muscles, only in the oldest of them was there a tendency to a permanent bandy stoop. And the older they were, the faster they shore and the simpler the job appeared. In the hands of the most experienced, the sheep seemed to be cooperating and turning itself to the blade.

"Wonnerful plant," conceded Ted. "Five hundred revs to the minute, the engineer tells me."

"Bit ahead of our chaps at home," said Hugh. "They still use hand shears. But they're pretty fast, too, with much bigger sheep than these merinos, and they don't cut 'em."

When I remarked on the big money the shearers earned Ted produced a book he had borrowed from the shed library. "Bin readin' poetry," he said with a grin. "Not my cupper tea, poetry. But this Australian stuff is suthink I can understand. Maybe not in the same class as Shakespeare—I wouldn't know. But listen to this—bloke called Lawson, Henry Lawson." And he read:

The old year went and the new returned, in the withering weeks of drought;
The cheque was spent that the shearer earned, and the sheds were all cut out;
The publican's words were short and few, and the publican's looks were black—
And the time had come, as the shearer knew, to carry his swag Out Back.

"And a lot more. It must be out o' date, fer I don't reckon none of these shearers will ever carry his swag. But good stuff, Bluey. Good poetry. Amazin' crowd, these Australians."

"Crude," remarked Hugh. "Elementary type of verse."

"Yes," said Hart, "but direct, simple, understandable and appealing to the emotions. At the same stage of development as Americans like Bret Harte in the 1850s, and for much the same reasons."

The quantity of liquid consumed by us all, shearers, rouseabouts and officials, was enormous. Tea and coffee (without milk, the tea strong, the coffee weak) was issued at every smoko and every meal, in big kerosene cans. Every man had his half-pint pannikin which he filled with

173

a dipper. In all, the cans of hot tea and coffee appeared eight times between getting up and going to bed, and most men drank a pint each time. The body needed it all.

With over a hundred men around, the shed was lively. The library hut was surprisingly well stacked, and mostly with classics and good modern books; and there was always auction bridge, cribbage and euchre, the sailors' card game, going at weekend. Most nights we turned in early, for the day was long and hard. Two-up, dice gambling and hard liquor were forbidden.

During the second week the news spread around that Hulton Sams was coming out on the Sunday. He came. The Reverend Hulton Sams—probably the most famous name in all western Queensland. Every man, including the cooks, packed into the library shed when he drove up in his buggy and changed in the woolclasser's quarters.

When he entered the big hut greetings and handshakes accompanied him all down the hall to the little pulpit he had brought himself. Hulton Sams was a trim, handsome man, still not much more than thirty, sparish of build, and somewhere around ten stone. He led the enthusiastic singing, and the quiet during his prayers was just as astonishing to me as the interest shown in his brief but serious sermon to these hard men of the bush.

The service lasted about half an hour after which the Reverend Hulton Sams stepped down from his pulpit, threw off his surplice and produced two pairs of boxing gloves. He was dressed ready for the ring, in vest, shorts and boxing boots.

"Don't rush, lads," he said with a smile. "You can all have a shy at the old Aunt Sally."

They formed a ring and five hefty opponents tried their luck one after another without much visible success. They were bigger and stronger, but his shrewdly planted blows soon reduced them to slow moving targets. Hulton Sams was not simply a brilliant boxer; he also kept himself as fit and fast as a boxer needs to be.

The last to step forward, however, was young and smaller—much the same build as Hulton Sams himself.

"My name is Ryan of Barcaldine, sir," said the youngster.

"Ha! Old Mick's son?"

"Nephew. But I'm a pro. You're not allowed to box a pro, are you?"

"Well, come to that," said Hulton Sams, "I'm a pro myself—a professional parson, but I hope nobody here would mind if I buried him."

After the roars of laughter the two boxed a very keen, scientific three rounds.

Over the coffee and cakes around the cook's fire, Hulton Sams sought out the four of us immigrants.

"I'm from Sussex," he said. "And you?"

"London," I said.

"Me, too," said Ted.

"Bedfordshire," said Hugh.

The parson looked at Hart, who smiled sweetly and replied: "Weren't you in the Cambridge boxing team five or six years ago?"

"True. And you?"

I had the feeling these two instinctively knew they were meeting on equal footing in some way and that the parson was challenging rather than inviting Hart to discuss it.

"I was always interested in amateur boxing," said Hart, and so adroitly switched the conversation to Hulton Sams' own life in the west that it stayed that way until the classer and the squatter claimed him and took him off to dinner.

CHAPTER NINETEEN
Big job—cook's slushy

SO WE CUT OUT at Aramac and followed the mob around the circuit—Acacia Downs, Barcorrah, Paradise Downs, Barcaldine Downs. Hugh and Jack Hart earned big money as wool pressers, which was a contract job. They filled the great bales from the bins, one carrying armfuls of fleece while the other stamped the wool down. They worked together on the hand press until the bale stood, like a huge sugar cube, stuffed hard as a rock.

With their bale hooks they rolled the bales away to the marker who dabbed the brand mark on them, and they were ready for the wool wagons to take them either to the wool scour or to the railhead for the coast, England and the Bradford sales. Old hands told us the traditional yarns of queer discoveries said to have been made when the bales were opened at Bradford, including a cook who forgot the salt in the stew.

Ted became automatically the honorary librarian at each shed, for which he was always voted at the closing meeting an honorarium of five pounds. He also made himself useful to the engineer and was never tired of discussing machinery. His experience in London, though personally limited, enabled him to see how two or three operations could be rolled into one with the right type of mechanical aid. The librarian job which he made his own rankled with me in an odd way, for I felt I must be better equipped to do it yet hadn't had the acumen to get it.

I stumbled into the big money when our cook's slushy (officially known as cook's offsider) went crook with a nasty bite which bush methods could not cure and had to be put on Cobb's Coach to Longreach Hospital. The cook offered me the job, which I accepted at once. It wasn't more arduous than most bush jobs, but it lasted eighteen hours a day, almost without a break. I ate while I worked.

Our cook was paid five shillings a head by the squatter and had to make the best of the food supplied him. He paid his slushy a third, and as there were between sixty and eighty rouseabouts to feed my share was enormous, at least five pounds a week, sometimes seven.

At four o'clock in the morning I had a dig from the cook, who turned over for another hour while I climbed out into the darkness, stirred the embers of the big open fire into life, and built it up with logs. Swinging from chains over the fire were the iron boilers, each holding several gallons of water which had to boil in time to make the tea and coffee ready for half past five, early morning smoko.

At six o'clock the cook appeared, scrubbed his head in ice-cold water, donned an immaculate white apron and hat, and proceeded with the breakfast. For this he required large beds of red-hot coals from the burning wood. From his butcher's shop he brought out the meat.

The meals never varied. When the sheep were slaughtered each day the chops were put aside for breakfast, the shoulders boiled for dinner and the legs roasted for "tea". Off-cut meat was minced into meatballs the size of cricket balls, the small chops were bread-crumbed and became cutlets, and the big chops were grilled.

The grilling was quite simple: a handful of salt thrown on the coals to kill the flames, green twigs laid across, and the chops laid on the twigs. Two pounds of meat was about the average put on a tin plate for breakfast, but one could have twice the quantity and it wouldn't arouse any comment.

For me, as slushy, having made the tea and coffee again, the job was the laying and clearing of the tables and the washing up of the pannikins, tin plates, and knives and forks, washing over the tables, getting more logs for the fire, more water for the boilers, making more tea and coffee for mid-morning smoko and staggering up to the shed with the four-gallon cans. The problem was to get each job done in time to start the next, for the shed worked by the clock, men were tired, thirsty and hungry, and there were eight meals or smokos each day.

I was expected to find time during the morning to help the butcher skin, clean and dress the sheep after he had killed and bled them, and in the afternoon the cook felt I should be interested in his special method of making highly valued delicacies for Sundays, brawn and pressed offal. The brains, liver, kidneys and tongues were preserved in brine each day for this purpose. The cook made a batch of yeast bread every morning, and cakes with currants on Sundays. He earned his money. So, I thought, did I.

My day ended with cleaning away after bedtime tea and coffee, and I tried to be in bed by ten but seldom achieved this. Of course, I had no time for books or cards nor for anything more than a "How's it goin'?" for my stable mates. I was perpetually short of sleep. But, financially, cook's offsider was my best job yet and I hung on to it as long as I could.

It ran out inevitably when my cook went on the booze between sheds and was in gaol when he was due at the next shed. Another cook was found, and he brought his own slushy. In time, just as inevitably, the new cook would have gone on the booze and my man would have got his place again in the circuit. Boozing was a routine hazard for the bush cook.

HUGH AT LAST had a reply from his father, who apparently thought the idea of buying a share in a farm to grow pineapples was sheer madness. Who would eat so many pineapples, he asked? But he did not suggest that Hugh should come home. He asked for more details without offering any hope of supplying the cash.

Hugh was indignant. "He forced me to emigrate for the sake of the family name, though if what I heard was true he'd been in a good many scrapes himself with women and girls—still keeps a mistress."

"So what will you do?" asked Hart.

Hugh was quite decisive. "I'll write again. Either he pays or I go home. And by golly if I go home I'll sleep with every girl in the village. I'll tell him that, too. The bloody old hypocrite. I'd like to see him out here in the west working for his living with not a woman in sight.

"He condemns me to live out here because I took a girl. She wasn't a virgin. But there was a row. I'd just like to have the old whoremonger out here in the bush with his tongue hanging out like a dog for the sight of a female."

"I seem to remember you had a pretty good opinion of the girls in Rockhampton," said Ted drily.

"Yes. But I wasn't brought up to earn a living like this. He knew that. He knew I'd have to live rough and use my muscles. Not that I mind that, for a while. But not for ever. This sort of life to me is simply filling in until I get settled in near a decent community, where there's dancing and restaurants and laundries and fun on a Sunday afternoon."

I was watching Hart to see how he reacted to this unexpected outburst. He looked away at the dusty horizon reflectively, and then stood up and said: "I think I'll wash my pants."

I felt a sense of something crumbling. In England, my family life, and that of other families I knew, was organised on rigid Methodist lines. You had to love your father or go to hell. Now I was learning about other sorts of families.

LIFE NEVER WENT smoothly for very long in the bush, but we four managed well enough while the shearing season lasted, with short occasional laying off periods. Hart paid his Rockhampton debts and looked happier for it, and during one stagnant fortnight Hugh was on the point of leaving for the coast and home when Bannister dropped in and offered us all jobs on his shearing contracts around the small squatters.

This was something different, for we travelled on his wagons, pitched our tents and erected the small shearing plant in the open, building cover from the sun with bush and scrub. Our six shearers would clear the mob in a fort-night, and we all fell on the job of dismantling like ants and were away the same night, sleeping in the wagons

179

on the way to the next selection. A bit elementary, but more like a large family affair.

We worked whatever hours were necessary, turned our hands to any job to make the contract work out successfully. Bannister fed us well. Ted proved of immense value with the plant, and I found the shearers not above letting me have a go with shearing a sheep during smoko, and giving me coaching, though shearers were very cautious about letting newcomers into their highly-paid craft.

Bannister's daughter Katey was often with us, keeping the books. She was a quiet, tidy-looking girl of twenty, a fine picture on a horse, and I was flattered when she invited me to go riding with her on Sundays. We sat and talked as we ate our food in the shade, and the conversation was always about us four Englishmen. I could never steer it over to her life. She had lived nowhere other than Western Queensland and had the dimmest idea of life in England, or even of life in Brisbane.

"Don't you want to see the world outside the west?" I asked her.

"Not particularly," she said.

In fact, it wasn't so much England that interested her as what we all did in England, what relations we had, whether we would go back, and to what. I thought about her once or twice and wondered whether I could marry her. It was merely speculative, for my experiences in the sugar country had let some daylight into my brain on the economics of being married on casual labourer's pay. I found her a very pleasant companion but was never tempted to make a pass. She didn't appear to expect it, which I found a relief but disappointing.

Ted, being odd-job man on the plant, had to learn to keep the books when Bannister's daughter wasn't with us and I didn't envy him the job. But he liked it. He liked any job which enabled him to learn something. Someone or other was saying "Ted around?" "Seen Ted?" twenty times a day, and little old Ted, with his slightly bowed shoulders and his habit of peering rather than looking, was here, there and everywhere, his Cockney nasal accent cutting

180

the air above the whine of the machines. He used to sing for us at nights, though the Australians could make no sense of the words of the old Gus Elen and Harry Champion songs.

Hugh said one night: "If I don't get a letter by the time we finish this group of selections I'm off home."

"What a pity," I commented. "If you stick at this wool-pressing you'll earn enough yourself for the fruit farm partnership."

"A thousand pounds? Not in a thousand years. Besides, he ought to pay! He ought to pay!" His tone was so bitter that I disliked him. But it was true we weren't really getting anywhere. There was no goal for any of us, even in the dim distance, which would answer the problem of the future. Being employed was merely keeping alive.

We were shearing near Blackall when a cop rode up one Saturday afternoon, on his monthly tour of the tracks in this vicinity. We all crowded round him for news and mail. But he had no mail.

"Just passing," he said over a billy of tea and a cold shoulder of mutton. "By the way, Mr Bannister, you got some English coves with you?"

We four stepped forward. "News?"

"Not exactly. It's just that we had a message about a missing person. We get 'em ten a week. They send the same message to every station house in Australia, on the off chance. Nothing we can do about them. But this one we have to ask about. Feller called Wendell. Ever heard the name?"

All looked blankly. "Well, it was a million to one shot," said the cop. "They don't even know for sure what part of the world he's in."

Stupidly I said: "There was a Wendell Holmes, Oliver Wendell Holmes, but I don't suppose . . ."

"Could be. Could be a lead," the cop said eagerly. "What was he like? When did you last see him?"

"I didn't," I said. "I read him. He writes about break-fast."

The cop flushed with anger. "This isn't a matter to make

kids' jokes about. Wendell is wanted in your country for murder."

I tried to make amends with an apology but he ignored me and rode away, leaving me feeling exposed and foolish.

"Police," said Hart, "have no sense of humour. They can't afford to. If you make a cop look silly you're tearing his uniform off. And what's a cop without a uniform?"

"I vaguely remember the Wendell case," said Hugh. "Just before we came out. The chap killed a man who attacked his sister."

"But wouldn't a man be acquitted in those circumstances?" I asked.

"It was a particularly vicious type of murder, I seem to remember," said Hugh.

Ted thought Wendell would have got away with ten years, maybe seven if rich enough to afford an expensive lawyer.

What occurred to me at the time was the remarkable absence of crime in the bush, yet with scarcely one policeman per five thousand square miles. I once heard of the shooting of a shearer while he was shearing, but it appeared that the man who killed him was out of his mind at the time. Assault, generally while drunk, was the most serious charge the bush town magistrates usually had to decide, the rest being petty offences such as train jumping and two-up in the street.

The unmarried men in the bush country—and very few bush wanderers seemed to have a home to keep— were satisfied to work hard, take their cheques to a town, and spend the lot on booze and such available women as there might be. Out on the job they talked of big things, down south, Brisbane, Sydney, Melbourne, when they took their cheques, but for many their thirst was too great. It pinned them down at the nearest pub.

CHAPTER TWENTY
Hugh gets his chance

HUGH GOT his next letter from home shortly afterwards. The Australian postal service had done a great job in delivering it, for Hugh was the sort of careless devil who never bothered to leave a forwarding address but expected the post people to perform miracles. The letter was three months old but the contents were worth waiting for. Hugh's face, as he read it, was a study in changing emotions.

"I . . . I've misjudged the old boy," he said finally, with a queer break in his voice. "Being stuck out here, I suppose it's made me an unpleasant bastard. Though apparently . . ."

"Oh I don't know," said Hart. Hart never could stand emotional display. Now he tried to kill it with quiet irony. "What does he say, anyway?"

"Well, I'll read it to you," Hugh answered.

He decided he wouldn't read the first paragraph, started the second and changed his mind and eventually began on the second page: "I ask you to believe that I never intended to banish you from England and our family for all time. I sent you to rough it for a while because I honestly believed you needed shaking up. The affair of the girl was of no consequence. It happens to most young men. But you were getting bumptious, lazy, selfish and deceitful and it grieved me. I knew you had the right stuff in you and the fact that you were being spoiled was not entirely your fault.

"You've served your sentence and now you shall have the choice of coming home, or of taking this partnership in fruit growing out there. But there's no hurry, because I am coming out myself. If you decide to come home, I hope you will agree that we can travel home together and perhaps establish the sort of understanding we have always needed. But if not, then I will go with you and see the place. Don't forget, old chap, that we have been farmers for generations. I may be able to make suggestions as well as find the money."

Hugh looked up from the letter. "There's some more which is a bit private, and he says at the end that he will send a cable when his ship leaves."

"So you're going 'ome," Ted's voice was gritty. "Back to the big 'ouse with servants to saddle yer 'orse and clean yer boots, and the villagers will say yessir and nossir and tip their caps when you go by. Eggs and bacon fer breakfast in bed an' church on Sunday mornin' in the private pew: you bet you're goin' 'ome."

Hugh was shocked by this attack. We all were. Then Hugh said with a forgiving chuckle: "It isn't as grand as that, Ted. And I'm not at all sure I want that life again. I want the chance to build something with my own hands. Farming in England, well, you make a living under the Conservatives and you go broke when the Liberals get in. But on the coast out here is virgin soil where I can make anything grow. Packing and marketing are the problems."

"Remarkable what a letter does to a man's outlook," said Hart. But there was no sarcasm in his voice; rather perhaps wistfulness. I had never seen Hart get a letter from home.

Hugh agreed eagerly. "Funny thing about my old man. I don't really dislike him but I don't think I've ever known him. Never had much opportunity, what with being at boarding school since I was eight, and afterwards he was usually out on the farm or at the sales or a meeting in London. He gave me what I wanted and snarled at me when I did something he didn't approve of—after all, I'd only left school two years when this trouble occurred and he shipped me out here before I realised what was happening. He's almost a stranger."

"Or you are," I suggested.

"No," said Hart. "I expect he knows his son pretty well, and maybe he's come to the conclusion recently that he hasn't made a friend of a growing-up son as he should have done. Now he is going to put the whole thing straight.

184

Well done, Hugh, and congratulations."

Ted and I mumbled something similar.

"Thanks," said Hugh. "What's your old man like, Jack?"

"I haven't got one," answered Hart. He smiled pleasantly as he said it, but one knew that further questions were not invited.

Only a few days after the letter came the cable, which said that Hugh's father was due in Brisbane in four weeks' time.

"I shall go right away," Hugh decided. "I need time to go and see the fruit farm again. No use taking the old man all the way up from Brisbane unless the offer's still open and the place looks a possibility. Besides . . ."

"Quite so," said Hart.

"Don't blame you," said Ted.

"Have a good time," said I.

"Well," Hugh admitted, "we've been out in the west a long time. I'm glad of the excuse."

So we had a parting session in a Blackall boozer and saw him off on the train to the coast. I expected Hart would go with him, but he preferred to stay with us. "For a while," he said.

There was a letter from Hugh several weeks later. It was a happy letter. His father had done a good deal of research before leaving England on north Queensland coastal farming, and marketing prospects He thought the partnership was good enough only as a means of learning all there was to know, and that something bigger and better could follow. In fact his father appeared to be even more enthusiastic than Hugh.

This letter had a profound effect on the three of us.

"That's one of us settled," I said, and was bitterly conscious of the fact that my own prospects were entirely non-existent.

"Lucky bastard," was Ted's comment.

"Because he's got a rich father?" queried Hart. "I suppose so. Though I'd die of boredom if I had to live my life on a fruit farm outside a little town."

185

"How can you say that?" I expostulated. "Out here we don't even work near a little town, and we certainly don't have the food and comfort of the coast, nor can we ever start a sheep station. Our only change from camp life is to stay in a pub somewhere. There may not be any real future, any way of building up something, either in the bush or on the coast but at least on the coast you don't have to stand on a dead sheep to get some slimy water out of a billabong."

"All very true," agreed Hart. "But what you say only applies to the bushwhackers like us. Out here there is a good and interesting life if you can find it. They're always doing something new on these big sheep stations, fighting disease, breeding for better wool, sinking artesian bores and digging bore drains to beat the droughts, and they have race meetings and breed horses to race and to ride, and draught horses for the wagons. The squatters build themselves fine houses and grow plantations around them and their wives grow flowers. Oh, I know life is elementary, but that's unimportant if it's interesting and creative."

"And if it gets you somewhere," Ted added. "But 'ow does a bloke get the chance? Not by this bleedin' rouse-about work."

"It'll come, it'll come," said Hart. "We've all got brains, we're young, and we've all got to keep our eyes open. With all its flies and heat and droughts this bush country must have a big future once its chief problems of water and transport are solved."

"Will they ever be solved?" I wondered.

"Money will solve any problem if there's money to be made," was Hart's answer.

All that Hart said made sense, but offered no clue so far as I was concerned, and this I pointed out.

"Unfortunately," said Hart, "you were the most useless sort of immigrant to this country. You had no knowledge of anything of value out here. Hugh is a farmer and ought to have gone straight into farming country. Ted understands machinery and electricity. I am something of an expert on horses and I know a bit about animals generally.

186

We will fit in. But you, my dear Bluey, have nothing except labouring, which is badly paid and over-supplied.

"But," he added, seeing the depression on my face, "you are young, fit, you have learnt to live hard and you are learning to use your brains. I know what I'd do in your shoes."

"What would you do, Jack?"

I was afraid he was going to say: "Go home." But he didn't. He said: "Hugh will help you once he's settled. He's a real good sort at heart. Ask him if he can give you a job —a permanent job which will enable you to study the *business* of fruit farming. You can make yourself a valuable man in a few years, and as our old Cockney friend at Mackay once told you, there are plenty of other ways of getting ahead down there on the coast, on the business side of life."

This was exactly what I wanted to be told. As I grew up, so my dreams faded. Yet the more realistic outlook was worth fighting for. But one had to keep an eye open always for the chance. Hart apparently thought I had something, though when I started to wonder what it was I had I felt depressed.

CHAPTER TWENTY-ONE
And Ted gets his

THE CREEK AT Muttaburra, which you cross as you come in from Bowen Downs, is dignified by the name of Thomson River. The Thomson starts as a chain of waterholes further north by Hughenden, is joined around and below Muttaburra by various creeks and dry courses, meanders through the flat country of gidya scrub and turkey bush to Longreach.

Here it is joined by the Barcoo from Barcaldine and by various nameless, waterless riverbeds; then it changes its name to the more colloquial one of Coopers Creek and looks like being quite important for several hundred miles until it finishes ingloriously in a lake in South Australia. However, the Thomson does have a beginning and an ending, which cannot be written of most rivers on the map of central Australia.

To the newcomer, arriving weary and parched at one of these creeks to find it bone dry, without sign of life except the inevitable crow on a leafless tree, it is one more bitter reminder that nature has not prepared this country for habitation by civilised humans.

But if he stays until it rains—and this may mean years —he will see that these dry watercourses at least have a function. They carry off the floods. They also perform a sort of irrigation, though it seems to be one of nature's accidents. In fact this is a momentary affair, for the flood waters vanish into the earth and within a short space of time the creeks are dry again. Only waterholes remain.

Muttaburra was our centre occasionally. It is the hub of the sheep country and on the fringe of the vast cattle plains back in the Never-Never. No railroad goes to Muttaburra: it lies between Winton, which is the end of the line out from Townsville, and Longreach, which is at the end of the line out from Rockhampton. One step over the bridge on the Thomson and you were on a bush track.

Some of the largest sheep stations in the world used Muttaburra for supplies which came in by wagon from one of the railheads, and also for casual labour, for domestic stores, saddle and harness repairs, blacksmithery, police (to be avoided if at all humanly possible) and for the pubs. The pubs were the most important of Muttaburra's industries.

There was one main street leading up from the creek with pubs on both sides and some stores and stables, and at the back of one side of the main street were the police station and magistrates' court. That was practically all there was of Muttaburra. The great wool carrier teams passed through Muttaburra on their way to the railhead. There were still one or two bullock teams but most were teams of powerful horses urged on by the crack of the long stock whips.

I had my twentieth birthday in Muttaburra, and about that time I had another anxious letter from my father who pointed out that I had been away well over four years and had made no progress. He was uneasy because he was afraid I was falling into bad ways and wicked company. He didn't actually write this, but he warned me, as he had done repeatedly, that the world was full of temptation and wickedness.

How odd it was, I thought at the time, that my father, a generous and God-fearing man, should live in the greatest and most enlightened city in the world, yet be so narrow-minded, while out here in the Never-Never township of Muttaburra all men drank and swore and fought and gambled, yet in a broader context they were honourable, hardworking men whom you could trust with your horse.

It was impossible to explain this to my father and I did not bother to try. I simply replied that I would probably be back in the sugar country within a couple of months and they were not to worry. "It takes time to settle in out here," I wrote, and repeated much of what Jack Hart had said. I also suggested that I was now almost fully grown and capable of minding my own morals, but about this I

189

was very gentle lest I offend the old boy.

The last time I came into Muttaburra I came without friends, and a tragic journey it was. Ted had decided to go on with Bannister to Barcaldine at his request and overhaul the plant during a slack period in shearing. Ted was not happy about the separation, but it was evident the pull to Barcaldine was too strong. He was happy with machinery and never swore at it. Hart was in and around Muttaburra. He never said how he earned his living.

For my part, I was the happiest man alive. I had bought a horse, saddle, bridle, blanket and hobbles. It was a three-year-old chestnut colt, and we chummed up from the moment I had my feet in the stirrups, shook the reins gently on his neck and said softly: "Let's get on, old boy." I called him Conkers. He had a sensitive nose and his mouth had not been ruined during the breaking. With a sturdy chest, clean hocks and smooth bright coat he looked a gentleman, yet just right to carry a young man and his swag.

I rode him several times and eventually bought him for nearly six months' pay, and when we cut out I decided to take the cross-country tracks to Muttaburra, to find Jack Hart. I had nothing against going to Barcaldine, but I wanted the longer ride to show Hart my horse.

As I rode along I sang. I was wildly happy. Conkers was the first real possession of my life. Except for childhood toys I had never owned anything, and here I was now, with the lovely animal responding to every touch of the reins; his ears pricked up to the note in my voice. My swag, which I had humped so many miles, lay across the saddle with my tucker and waterbags hung close, and it occurred to me that Conkers was as pleased with me as I was with him.

At the end of the second day I pulled in under some trees where there was water nearby and a patch of green grass, around an overspill from a bore drain.

"Fancy finding that," I said to Conkers. "This looks like the real stuff, like we have back home."

190

So I led him to it, hobbled him and set about making a fire for myself.

In the morning Conkers was not well. His head hung, he coughed, and his eyes were wild. I took off the hobbles and watered him, but it was evident I had a sick horse and no medicine, nor horse knowledge. I kept him in the shade all that day, soothed him and talked to him, and prayed for someone to come by. Conkers lay down, and I knew then that he was bad. I was frantic but quite helpless.

On the following morning the crows were gathering, and in the afternoon Conkers died. It was not a pretty sight.

Never in my life had I experienced such grief, for within a few days Conkers had become the dearest and most deeply loved possession I had ever known. I was twenty and a man—but I wept like a kid.

In the bush even such a tragic happening as this, the worst in my life at that time, did not render one so helpless with shock and sorrow as it would in a community. With no one to turn to for help, the situation demanded decision and action. I had to get somewhere and now I had a saddle and bridle as well to carry. And I had the ghastly problem of what to do about Conkers.

Burying a horse is a job for six men with spades. I had no spade. I thought that with luck I could reach a sheep station next day and perhaps get a lift on from there, or sell the saddle and walk on; but leaving Conkers to the crows was unthinkable, if inevitable.

I threw sticks at them when they came too close with their gluttonous squawks, made up the fire for the night, and just before sundown an old buggy arrived. A north of England voice greeted me.

The stumpy Geordie jumped down and quenched his thirst at the waterhole.

"So we're both from t'Old Country? What's to do with the horse?"

"I don't know," I said miserably. "He just died."

The Geordie looked him over. "Stummick," he said. "Poisoned."

191

I shook my head. "No poison here. Just good green grass."

"Ah," said the Geordie. "That's it. What they call the scours. These horses never see green grass. They live dry —this blue Mitchell grass and scrub leaves."

His matter-of-fact attitude helped me and next day he took me on into Muttaburra and drove into the pub where I usually stayed. I helped him with his horses, and noticed a large box, almost the size of a coffin.

"That box, lad?" He chuckled. "That's my tools. Carpenter and joiner."

Hart came in from the two-up school down by the creek and listened to my grievous story. He didn't commiserate. On the contrary, he asked a few questions and then commented: "Well, you've lost a good horse and you've learnt a lesson. But you've got a good deal more to learn before I trust you alone with a horse. Horses are the finest creatures God ever made. They carry us around, pull our wagons and our ploughs, race for us, and never complain or give up, even though sometimes they're kicked and thrashed. In wars they die for us. But they also depend on us for food and water and to keep them healthy. It's little enough to do in return."

I left him without replying, feeling the salt stinging in the wound, and went out deliberately to get drunk. It wasn't easy until I mixed whisky with the beer.

Several hours later, finding my way back in the darkness to my own pub, I heard a horse sneeze, and staggered into a stable and started to stroke the horse's nose and chatter with him, and I could remember next morning that a cove with a hurricane lamp had said: "Fine horse, mister. You want to buy him?"

After a short harangue I satisfied my ego by buying the horse and to hell with Hart and his lectures. I paid the joker eight pounds, which he accepted after having first asked thirty-five.

Hart had the story out of me next morning and together we went to see the horse. It was a walking hat-rack, down at one hip and at least sixteen years old according to Hart after examining its teeth.

"I'll soon put some flesh on him," I said. "Good food is what he needs."

"You'll not put an ounce on him," Hart answered. "He's too old. In fact your only chance is to find another drunk tonight who is stupid enough to buy a horse by hurricane lamp. Personally I'd give him back and cut the losses."

Eventually I did. I was disliking Hart quite a lot just then. Instead of sympathy I had met cold hostility and severe rebuke. To Hart the death of a fine young horse was itself the tragedy. My own loss and grief were an insult to Conkers.

Back at the pub the Geordie stood me a pint. The bar was empty except for Sam, the big paunchy publican, and us.

Sam leaned heavily over the bar. "You a carpenter?" he said.

"Aye."

"You want a job?"

The Geordie laughed derisively. "A job? In this 'ole? Ah'm driving out the night."

Sam was not easily beaten. "You can earn a hundred quid in less'n a fortnight," he said. "Matter of puttin' up a bungalow down be the creek. All the stuff's there—joists, iron sheeting, plates. What's more, the piles are driven in and levelled. It don't really need a builder, but I want this done in style. You ever put up a house, chum?"

The Geordie said he'd built houses all over Lancasheer, Chesheer and Yorksheer, even in Derbysheer—"but real houses." Only the carpentry and joinery, of course. But real carpentry. "Not like these dumb hen-coops they call houses out here. Any fool could tack 'em together. But there's no satisfaction in a job like that. Know what I mean?"

I agreed. "But," I added, "it's a lot of dough."

"Aye," he reflected.

Sam put a packet on the counter. "Plans," he said. "Bluey knows the place. Show our friend the site, Bluey."

The Geordie regarded the bottom of his tankard, deep in thought. "It could be done," he said, "if I had me mate. I can't work without a mate."

Sam looked at me.

"Sure," I said.

"You know owt about this work?"

"Enough. What do I get?"

"You get a third," said Sam. Good old Sam. He had a soft spot for me. I liked Sam, too. I knew why this bungalow was so important to Sam. Sam had a love affair over at Winton, a fine upstanding barmaid who would one day be as fat as Sam. Worth going all the way to Winton, and then having to hang around until she closed the bar and was free to go to bed—"But I got me business. So finally we figured we'd get married. I was reckoning on Jennie working here then, but Jennie wants it all on the line, house'n'all, and no more beer-pulling, so she'll be fresh when I come round. I thought that was nice of Jennie. But she won't come to Muttaburra until the bungalow's up."

The Geordie was undecided, so I picked up the plans, took him by the arm and led him down the street to the bridge over the Thomson and turned left to Sam's plot. It was on the top of the bank, overlooking the creek, with a few gums and scrubby trees around. The piles had all been driven and trued, and beside them was the pile of sawn timber and iron—a package house all ready to assemble.

We sat in the shade and I spread out the plans.

"Looks fairly simple," I suggested, but in fact I'd never seen a plan before.

"Kid's stuff," said the Geordie contemptuously.

The publican followed us down. He was sweating profusely.

"What's this contraption?" the Geordie asked him.

"The galley."

"Cookhouse," I added.

"Ah." The Geordie was interested at last. "No kitchen in this house?"

Sam looked at him in astonishment. "This pot of pink paint," he said. "I've ordered it specially for the bedroom.

194

That's the bedroom." He planted a stubby finger on a space in the centre of the house. It was, so far as I could see, the only room, and it had no windows.

"Bit 'ot for sleeping, won't it be?" said the Geordie.

Sam was getting hot, but he remained patient. He was very anxious to get this house built. I suspected he was finding the journey to Winton once a fortnight a bit too much, even for Jennie's love.

"We ain't goin' ter sleep in it," he said. "You paint it pink, and I'll have a big double bed with sheets and blankets and one o' them coloured quilts, and a dressing table—and a picture of the King or somethin'. Ladies like that sort of thing."

"But," said the persistent Geordie, "what's the bed for?"

Sam was slightly nonplussed. "It might be cold enough one night to sleep in it instead of on the verandah; but you can't have a bedroom without a bed in it, and Jennie wants a bedroom. This is going to be a real bosker, the whole thing, with flowers . . ."

"Flowers?" I said, startled, looking around the tangle of weeds and rocks.

"Yair," he persisted. "Flowers. I seen 'em grow in Longreach and I reckon Jennie'll grow 'em in Muttaburra. Youse boys get the house up."

As he turned to leave, the Geordie said: "I shall want to draw summat. For tobacco and such."

Sam nodded and left.

I took up the plans. "What do we do first?"

The Geordie stretched himself at full length under the gum. "Best start with the cookhouse," he said. "That'll be shade for me tools and for smoko and such. Get the stuff for the cookhouse ready and then go and fetch me box of tools."

I hesitated. These orders were a bit unexpected. But, I reassured myself, probably that was what carpenter's mates were expected to do. Either way it was a lot of money.

The vast, glittering array of tools in the Geordie's tool-

195

box was a constant source of excitement to me—the saws, chisels, braces, screwdrivers, hammers, and lesser-known implements. Building the house wasn't difficult, for a while. The big plates were all the right length when laid over the piles and nailing them on was enjoyable work. The floor joists fitted over the piles and the flooring nailed down nicely onto the joists.

The Geordie's idea of putting up the galley first proved to be a good one, especially for the Geordie. It provided shade when we knocked off for a spell, and the Geordie believed in plenty of spells. I had only to ask him whether he was married or if he'd eaten pawpaw and it was a certainty the Geordie would say: "Oh, ah. Well, now, let's knock off for a spell, lad."

He let me do most of the work, which was too element-ary for a master carpenter and which I enjoyed doing, so that the galley proved its value as a handy place from which the Geordie could supervise while stretching full length.

From the floor upwards the job became less easy. To fit the uprights into the horizontals, the instructions were to mortice them, which meant chiselling out square holes and shaping the timber ends to fit into the holes. This I felt the Geordie should do and said so, having botched up a couple of attempts myself.

"Old fashioned and unnecessary," he declared. "Just get some good nails and nail 'em in."

Having got them to stand up he had another good idea —to strengthen the whole structure at this stage by nail-ing the sheets of iron on the sides to make the walls. I must say this worked very well, and without this support I could never have proceeded with the roof at all.

"Y'can't expect me to be interested in work like this," said the Geordie, "but I'll keep thee straight and mebbe you'll learn summat before job's done."

In the middle of the job Ted arrived at Muttaburra, without warning. It had been a two-day train and coach journey. He looked fit and alert, however, and he had new clobber.

196

"You got the sack?" were my first words, after greeting.

Ted paid for two pints and led me to a quiet corner.

"Bluey, old pal," he said, "I've 'ad a very important offer."

"Well, that's good news," I exclaimed, impressed by his very serious expression. "Am I in on this?"

"It's Bannister," he said. "He's got a great chance to expand—get bigger contracts. But he's got no idea of organisation. He can look at a mob and price the cost of shearing, or even buy the clip itself. But buying plant, keeping books, feeding the camp, running to schedules, all that scares the pants off of 'im. And now Katey don't wanter keep the books no more."

"Katey?"

"Yus. Bannister's daughter. Well, the thing is, old sport, Bannister's offered me six quid a week permanent. All the year, and a quarter profits. Sorter junior partner."

I gaped, astounded. Ted? Junior partner?

" 'Course," he added quickly, "you'd have to be in on it. I said: 'Well, there's my pal Bluey,' I said. 'We bin pals now nigh on four years,' I said. And that's what I came over here to see you about."

I sat back, still flabbergasted. Then I came to my senses and said: "Why it's marvellous. It's what you've always wanted, Ted, something like this. What a chance!"

"I know." He wasn't smug, or self-satisfied. In some way he was almost humbled by this turn of fortune.

I knew in that moment that Ted and I were splitting. Ted had found what he had been groping for all his life. In all his thirty years he had struggled in the undergrowth of humanity for a place in the light. Dispensable. Paid by the hour, fired by the hour. In another five years he would have given up the struggle.

Here was the chance he wanted. He would never let it go. This was why he had come to Australia, for back in England he was doomed, before he was born, to live his life submerged. Ted would be a good assistant contractor. Ted would get to know every detail of the business, from finding the best cook and woolclasser to seeing the wool

197

off to the railhead. Given the right field Ted was amazingly alert and intelligent. His smattering of engineering and electrical works were invaluable in a country of unskilled labour; and Ted could be tough. I could see him as a partner, a man of value, master of the economics of contracting, indispensable at last.

"You see," he said, as though explaining his luck, "I never did no bookkeeping in my life but any fool could see what a mess he'd made of it."

He waited for me to say something, and seeing the expectancy in his eyes I pulled myself together and said: "Ted, I'm glad. It's great. It's absolutely marvellous." He looked relieved until I added: "But Ted, honestly it's not for me. Knocking around little sheep stations wool rolling and penning up, and washing pants on Sundays, and never saving a sprat—no, I can't see it any more."

He was aghast. "But you're bound to get the same chance, Bluey, boy, either with us or maybe on a station. Bookkeeping, for instance."

"Never. I couldn't stick it if I did. Matter of fact I think you're going to find places like Blackall a dull sort of bushwhacker's paradise to enjoy life waiting for the next shed."

I wished I could take those last words back. It sounded like sour grapes, as in fact it was, even though true enough. We were both sick of loafing around three-pub towns, and six-pub towns, sometimes one pub, hearing the same old bush yarns, watching the same sort of gambling, drunken fighting, eating burnt steak for breakfast, with an egg on it on Sundays, flies, flies, flies, warm flat beer the colour of mahogany . . . an occasional gamble to stave off the creeping paralysis of tropical boredom which holds a man down with unseen but ever strengthening bonds.

"Well," he said, "there's something else."

He stopped in his tracks. I waited.

"Let's get a coupla pints," he said.

This could only mean that further shocks were coming.

Ted knocked back his pint in a single swallow and wiped the sweat from his blinking eyes. Sometimes those little eyes were very black, very bright through the mistiness of short sight, but on rare occasions they were almost lost in their mist. That's how they were now, as he stuttered and stammered around. But eventually, it emerged, the stupendous, incredible fact. Ted had a girl. Bannister's daughter.

"Gawd knows what she sees in me, Bluey, but we get on fine and I've told her I'd ask her to marry me if I cud get meself a good job and she said that's fine, too, and how long would it have to be."

His agitation betrayed him into buying two more pints, while I sorted my thoughts from my feelings. It gave me a precious minute to steady myself. So, instead of telling Ted did he realise what a bloody fool he was, I said tamely: "Congratulations, old pal. I hope it turns out all right."

He looked wry. "Not exackly enthusiastic."

"Well," I said, "I do honestly hope it will."

"But you doubt it?"

"It's just that I can't see you settled down married and maybe with a family . . ."

"Why not? What's funny about that?"

"Nothing funny. But settling down for keeps, out here, for ever, for life! Not you, Ted. I don't see it. Still . . ."

"What makes you think I'm going to live here all my life? And what's up with life out here? You and me don't know how good it is when life is smooth, with a nice 'ouse an' garden . . ."

"Ted!" I almost shouted. "You can't even ride a horse!"

"I've thought about that," he said. "Anyone can learn. But there's another thing. Motor cars are coming. Mr Bannister has bought one."

"Motor cars? In the bush?"

"You'll see. Matter of fact I know a bit about petrol engines. It'll be another string to me bow. I could teach you, too, Bluey. In fact, we could work at it together." He was talking fast now, this inspired Ted whom I'd never seen before. "Might be a long time before the motor gets going out in these 'ere parts but it's bound ter come, like electricity. No roads? No. Well, they'll have ter make

199

roads. Some of the shearers already 'ave motor bikes, don't they? Anyway Bannister is using his car this season for me and the classer and 'im and the engineer."

The whole affair was too great a shock for me to understand fully what he was saying. It passed through my mind that I had never ridden in a motor car and I recalled my first ride in a motor bus from King's Cross to Finsbury Park and feeling very sick as the bus swayed past the horse trams, the frightened horses and the cursing drivers. It wasn't so long ago.

But this was so very unimportant.

Ted was saying: "Bluey, we must stick together, and see it through. We always said we would. I've struck it first, but you'll strike it, too, and I'll never leave you till you do."

He was watching me closely, maybe uneasily, as I said slowly: "Ted, you're a real pal, always have been. I'm grateful. I'm really glad for your sake, terribly glad you've got this chance. Of course it's a shock and a surprise. Who'd have thought—I mean, out here in the Never-Never, it's the last place where you'd expect a chance to crop up."

His beady eyes were searching for a clue to what was coming.

"But we can't expect to stick together forever. After all, I'm twenty, a man, able to fend for my own tucker. One of us was bound to hit something before the other."

"But you'll take a job with Bannister, Bluey? I might get you in as a presser on contract, if you think you can do it."

I shook my head. To me, the partnership was finished.

"Ted, let's put it all out on the table. I'm fed up with the bush. I owe it a lot, in a way, because I've grown up out here. But it doesn't alter the fact that unless you have a big business, and even if you have, it's all a lot of nothing at the end. Work, sweat, flies and pubs. So I think I'll get out."

"To the coast?" His voice was harsh but his words

sincere. "Well, that's it. We'll go to the coast. To hell with Bannister."

And the girl? The love affair? The great chance? What I said next was said on the spur of the moment, to check him somehow, by any expedient, from rashly promising something he'd always regret.

"No, Ted," I said. "I'm joining up with Hugh. You've got your chance of a lifetime, and a girl to marry. Well, maybe I'll find both this time down in the sugar. That's final, Ted."

He was persuaded, late that night, reluctantly. But for Katey, in fact, he would never have agreed to part. There was something about Ted, an inborn loyalty, which raised him from being a little, insignificant person to a man of stature whose friendship was something to be highly prized.

Next morning, at six, he climbed onto the coach for Longreach and as I watched the spiral of dust fade over the flat horizon I wondered why I had torn a great hole deliberately in the fabric of my life. Was it jealousy? Perhaps. Was it bush sickness? Partly, yes. Anything else? Katey? No, not Katey, but possibly the prospect of seeing Ted settling down as a happy, busy married man, nailing up pictures in his own home, carrying a couple of kids around, driving his wife out in their own buggy.

All this added up to final separation: he, settled into his groove; I, still a bushwhacker. I felt a fog had been swept from my mind by my decision. I could now see the way ahead. So I thought.

I WENT BACK to the creek and the half-built bungalow, the Geordie and the plans. He was now shrugging the whole thing off, and I had trouble with him when I discovered that the sacred room which had been decorated with the flaming pink paint, stood complete with four sides and no door or doorway.

"If you don't get off your backside," I told him, "Sam is going to get annoyed at the delay and I shall tell him why and leave you to finish it."

He started to bluster, but I wasn't having it. I began to wonder whether he'd ever been a carpenter and told him so. The Geordie then scratched his head over the plans, found the missing door, and after I'd removed enough walling he fixed the hinges and lifted the door on, inside out and upside down.

Sam came down to look around next day and brought me a letter from the Old Country. I recognised my father's angular writing and opened it. It contained a post office draft for twenty-five pounds and a long epistle from my father who had a promise of an office job for me from some old political pal. He more or less ordered me to come home at once before I was too old to return to a proper life. He hoped the money he enclosed would be enough. It was all he could spare, he said.

Events seemed to be piling up: Hugh gone only a few weeks, Conkers dead, Ted talking of marriage and partnership, and now my father telling me to come home. I hadn't the slightest intention of going home to admit defeat. The peremptory command to return was amusing, though it would have been obeyed without question four years earlier, and the post office draft was upsetting. I knew my father was poor, always thrifty, saving desperately for old age and no pension, and that twenty-five pounds meant that he was badly worried about me.

It might be reasonable to go home for a spell and see them, and let them see me and realise that all was well with the sunburnt young man emerged from sickly youth. But not on his twenty-five pounds, and maybe only after a year or more, working with Hugh. I had to have something to show, I felt.

CHAPTER TWENTY-TWO
Hart goes. I go too

THE RAINS CAME a week or two later. The bungalow was all but finished, standing like an iron-clad box, glaringly new with the sun's rays burning off it, just above the creek some fifty yards north of the bridge.

When the rains came work was immediately impossible. Nothing could move. Low heavy clouds had appeared a couple of days earlier and the air was tense with compressed heat. Rumbles of thunder meant little, but the old boys had been saying that the drought was due to break any day. There had been someone in from the coast, too, who had said people were talking about the monsoons this time.

The clouds broke at six in the morning. It fell, they said, at an inch an hour. The noise on the iron roofs was like a brigade of machine-guns firing simultaneously and continuously. Everyone not already out got up and half dressed and went out to stand in the downpour for the sheer thrill of it. Men began to tell yarns of great droughts of the past, yelling to make themselves heard through the din.

They said that in 1907 there were children eight years old who had never seen rain. They told of great mobs of dying sheep sold at threepence a head, of frightful losses of sheep and cattle, of men trying desperately to shear sheep before they collapsed, of raging bush fires which destroyed the scrub—the only food left for cattle—and then of the rise of great torrents sweeping all before them.

Within an hour the road through Muttaburra was a river draining into the Thomson. The circular tanks which caught the roof water at every building were filling up. People were scuttering to and fro with stores, preparing for a seige.

"It could rain like this fer ten or fifteen days," said one

old westerner to me, "or it could finish in ten minutes."

All through that day the rain crashed down. Hart and his two-up pals started a hazards game in a back room and I sat nearby, watching between spasms of letterwriting. Hart usually won at hazards unless he had a bad run, because he knew the exact mathematical odds of throwing a seven against a six or a five, for instance, and in these bush schools the arithmetic was of a rough and ready, slightly inaccurate character.

I didn't play, though I loved the game and its excitement. But too much had happened for me to be able to get down to dice. So I wrote to Hugh, and I wrote to Ted, and I even wrote to the barmaid at Barcaldine. And when I could think of no one else to write to I wrote the difficult one to my Dad. This one wasn't easy, for I had to be nice, grateful, but firmly refusing. I told him I was posting the draft back home but promised I would come back some time but for a holiday only. I didn't mention Conkers. I couldn't mention Conkers to anyone. Fortunately Ted had been too concerned with his future and mine to remember to ask me about my wonder horse . . .

During the day people fought their way through floods into the township and others left to lend a hand to friends and neighbours who might need help. Those on the high ground would be safe, safe at least from the floods, but those on the level would soon be in trouble. And anyone living near the Thomson or any of the tributary creeks was in real danger.

On the third day there was a break, and people raced around the place. The police came and called for volunteers but neither Hart nor I had a horse and were declined. One cop mentioned to Sam that a Welshman had been brought in from the Hughenden track. He had been robbed and left in a bad way and was picked up by a boundary rider and nursed for three weeks.

"He is hardly conscious yet but we think he's telling us that his buggy and tools were pinched by an English feller. Mean anything to you, Sam?"

Sam looked at me.

"The Geordie," we said together.

I ran out to the stables. The old buggy was missing.

"The bastard," said the cop.

"My bungalow," muttered Sam. "It'll never be finished now."

"We'll get the bastard, Sam," said the cop. This was poor consolation to Sam.

I had a thought. "The Welshman! He must be the real carpenter!"

"Ah!" Sam ran his thumb around inside the top of his strides. This was a habit of Sam's and I could never be sure whether he did it because his strides were too tight or whether he was letting some air inside. Or possibly it helped him to think. He turned to the cop: "When will he be fit to work?"

"I'm not the doc," said the cop. "But could be another week. We shall want him around for a bit to charge the other feller."

"Ah," said Sam. "Could be another coupla weeks, fr'instance?"

The cop nodded.

"With a real carpenter," I said, " we could make a good job of it in two weeks."

Sam pulled three drinks, looking much happier, raised his tankard and said: "Good dropper rain."

Over the midday steak I was telling Jack Hart about it when a thought struck me and I jumped up from the table. "The tools!"

Hart shook his head slightly. "Either the Geordie's taken them, in which case you can't finish the house, or he hasn't, which means that you can. Even if he has, the police will get him before he reaches the railway, if ever he does in this rain."

"But," I almost shouted at him, "the tools are down at the bungalow!"

"Assuming," said Hart, "the bungalow is where you left it."

I hadn't thought of that. It made the recovery of the tools even more urgent.

205

"I'm going down to get them," I decided, and got up from the table.

He waved me down. "A few minutes will make no difference, Bluey. Let me finish my dinner quickly and I'll come with you."

I told Sam. "Ah," he said, which I interpreted as meaning: "Well done and thanks."

A strong wind had sprung up and cut through us freezingly as we came out of the pub onto the sidewalk. "Could mean it's passing on now," said a man, looking at the rolling masses of cloud. "But," he shouted after us, "there's a lot to come!"

We were soaked in the first ten yards and the wind blew us down the streaming road to the creek. Before we reached it I saw the flood, a swirling, yellow sea, filling the Thomson to the brim and lashing pieces off the bridge. Washing down with the flood, now submerged, now spinning in the foam, was a medley of debris: fencing posts, broken furniture, clothes, trees, dead sheep, a wallaby and smaller animals, a bullock, feet upwards and bloated bobbing gruesomely in the rushing waves. Snakes and toads clung to floating tree branches, and on the bridge posts stranded in the torrent smaller living things, ants and spiders and crawling things, had sought desperately to find something solid to cling to.

Sam's bungalow was in a bad way. The cookhouse had vanished entirely and the whole of the structure of the bungalow had collapsed sideways against a big gum. The waters lapped over the verandah and sudden bursts of water smashed against the iron walls.

"Where's the tools?" Hart shouted.

"I know," I shouted back and pointed to the interior of the leaning shed. It was my job to get them, I felt, and I started at once along the verandah, holding where I could. Hart shouted something to me but I was out of earshot and took no notice. It was in my mind that inside the tangle of iron sheeting and boards was the box of tools and that the most I could do would be to push it into as safe a corner as I could, away from the clutch of the swirling torrent.

How it happened I never knew, but without warning I felt myself practically picked up and thrown into the river, and within seconds I was submerged, came up floundering and choking, sputtering water out of my lungs, and was at once down again. I knew then that I was drowning. I could swim, but not particularly well, and I might have had a chance of survival if I had dived in deliberately and had known what I was doing.

In the event I was more than half-drowned immediately, and was fighting to get upwards to breathe, and not to swim. How far out I was carried I never knew, nor whether I had been seconds or minutes in the act of drowning, when I felt an arm under my chin from the back of me and at once fought frantically to clutch it.

From a long way off, it seemed, through my water-logged ears, I heard Hart shouting: "If you struggle I'll let you drown!"

It came to me very distinctly, one word at a time, and it took effect. I began to choke.

"Keep on your back and swim with your legs."

Well, I could do the back stroke. Waves crashed over us, floating logs hit us, but we made it. Or, I should fairly say, Hart made it, keeping an iron grip on me until we were near enough for a crowd of men to haul us out and lay us like corpses somewhere above the flood.

They pumped the water out of me and eventually hauled me to my feet.

"Where's Hart?" I said.

"Yer cobber? He got a bash on the head going in," a chap in a sou'wester bawled. "Dived bang on into a log. Buggered if I know how he stuck it after that. They've took him to the First Aid. Out to the world. Yer in luck, pal."

I staggered a few paces, felt better after a swig of Scotch from a friendly flask, and realised we weren't more than a hundred paces from the crumpled bungalow. I moved towards it, ignoring a warning shout to get back to the hotel, and found Hart's shoes and jacket. The jacket was blowing around, and there were papers scattering.

I picked up his pocket book, stuffed papers and cards back, among them a small photograph. It was of a young girl. The print was yellowing, but I could clearly read the writing on the back: "To big brother from little sister with love." This, too, I put into the wallet and staggered up the street to the hotel.

Hart was back in the world an hour or so later, drinking a large brandy, when I reached the First Aid. They had fixed a plaster over his left temple, and by the size of it the cut must have been a big one.

He was glad to see me, and relieved when I produced his coat and shoes and some dry clothing. I gave him the wallet and he looked through it at once.

"Muddy," he said. "Things blow around?"

"I picked up all I could find, Jack," I said.

He took out the picture, and looked at it for a moment.

"This too?"

I nodded.

"Thanks," he said, putting it away. "She was my sister."

I felt he expected me to ask questions, or at least to say "Was?", but I had already decided not to know or wish to know.

What I did say was: "I've got one myself. She'd be eight now. I had to push her around in a pram when she was a baby. Wonder if she remembers me?"

We walked back towards the hotel. I might have thanked him, but it was difficult to thank Hart. One never knew his motives for anything he did.

"Must have been a close thing for you as well as me," I said.

"Bit difficult," he admitted. "Just as well I'm a strong swimmer. How d'you feel?"

"Me? I'm fine," I said, surprised. "Why?"

"Well then," said Hart, "let's go down there again. They need all the help they can get."

A few days later the rains had gone, the creek was still

in spate, but the sky was a hard blue, and the plains were already green. Families who had lost everything were still being brought in. After the evening meal Hart said: "Bluey, I bought a horse yesterday, and soon I'll be moving out."

"Where to?"

He shrugged his shoulders. "Plenty of places I haven't seen. Still searching for God knows what," he said, with a touch of weariness beneath the cynicism. "I hope you'll team up well with Hugh, and it may be I'll drop in on you one day."

He took out his wallet. "I owe you twenty-two pounds. Here it is, Bluey. Just when you need it."

He handed me the money. I realised with astonishment that he must have kept a record of his borrowings.

"What about you?" I asked. "I'll have a bit to come from Sam for building his bungalow if it's ever finished."

"Me?" He smiled one of his rare smiles, and it seemed that his pale blue eyes filled with a deeper warmer blue. "You're a pretty good friend to have around, Bluey. I'm all right for money just now. The system has worked well."

"Well," I said awkwardly, "you've been a pretty good pal yourself, one way and another. In fact you all have."

I felt there must be more to say, but Hart was not the type who would carry on any discussion, or argument, or farewell talk. He lived his life within himself, and others —even his friends in adversity—always remained outside.

He closed the issue by saying: "Bed early for me. Goodnight, Bluey."

I thought about Hart long into the night. I thought of the man he might have killed in the Brisbane pub, of his wild gambling, his complete callousness in losing the money I had worked so hard for, his gentleness in helping me, the watchful eye I always felt whenever I might be running into trouble, his plunging into that raging torrent to save my life. I thought of the photograph in his wallet and wondered about his early life—why this cultured young man of many talents was wandering about the bush at all.

I was up and out at six next day. But Hart was already gone. Even saying goodbye was a waste of time, words and emotions to Hart. "Why do it?" he would have said.

Now I was alone again. Well, it had happened after four years of friendship, kicking around together in tough spots and happy moments. I went down to the creek to see just how bad a state the bungalow was in and found the box of tools floating. The creek was full but the torrent was sliding by more steadily. I saw a child's mattress go by and wondered about the fate of its owner.

I sat on the verandah with the sun blazing into my face from the east. Grass, trees, even little flowers were springing into life. The west was putting on its Sunday coat. But I repeated to myself that, as I had told Ted, it held no future for me. I had nothing to give the west, and there was no purpose in remaining.

As I walked back deep in my thoughts I heard my name called from the pub they called the "War Office". I turned and saw my former mate the cook.

"I got offered a job, Bluey," he said. "Sixty-odd to feed. Not too bad. You want to slushy for me?"

It was the first job in my life I turned down, and somehow I felt I'd grown an inch bigger for having been able to do so.

The Welsh carpenter was out and around, but we didn't fancy each other. I settled with Sam and caught the coach to Hughenden. There, feeling flush, I broke all the rules of bushwhacking finally and forever by paying my fare down to Townsville. It was a fifteen-hour run and I watched the bush with its squawking crows and its leaping kangaroos disappearing behind me with mingled feelings and memories, until it ended with the slagheaps of Charters Towers.

From Townsville, a port of much the size and character of Rockhampton, I knew I'd have to go south to find Hugh in the Proserpine, but first I bought myself a grip, dismantled my swag for the last time and packed all my worldly goods into the sophisticated bag.

It was about four in the afternoon when I stopped to

read a typewritten notice in a small office window. It read: "Coal trimmer wanted for S.S. *Bochum* sailing for Hamburg tonight at 6 p.m."

Impelled by sheer curiosity I stepped inside the office. Two men were standing there, in conversation, and one broke off to ask me what I wanted.

"Just wondering about the job," I said.

"You a seaman?"

"Not exactly."

The other man broke in, talking with a strong foreign accent.

"Haf you efer verked on a ship, shovelling coal?"

This time I couldn't lie.

"No, but I've worked on the fires in a sugar mill" I said.

He turned away in disgust, but changed his mind. "Your hands," he demanded.

He examined my palms for corns, looked me over from head to toe, and said to the agent: "I think I'll haf to take this vun. I'm four men short."

The agent produced a paper. "You've got the job," he said. "Sign here."

It dawned on me that I was deciding, without any previous thought, to go home! True, I had generally acted on impulse, but this time I hadn't even had the impulse.

I played for time. "This Hamburg. My home is in England."

"Well, you're not dumb," said the agent. "It's not all that far off your course."

I looked at the form, procrastinating. "What do they pay?"

"Six pounds a month."

The captain was getting impatient. The impulse smote me.

I signed, and an hour later I went aboard. It was the evening of July 17th, 1914.

FIVE MONTHS passed before I spotted Holyhead Light. The Great War started while the *Bochum* was passing the East Indies and changed her course to join the German

Pacific Fleet. Several weeks of acute loneliness followed now as we dodged the British and Allied warships through Pacific Island groups (I was the only Britisher aboard). There were a few hectic but choicely memorable days spent obtaining my pay from a savagely angry German consul at Manila, where I escaped, and then eleven weary weeks coaling a miserable, ancient meat packet from Hong Kong to Liverpool.

But it passed. I stepped out of the train in London on a bitter December evening, and, stone the crows, there was my little Dad, his spectacles dimmed with tears, with an overcoat in his arms—for me.

We asked Harold Lewis to send us some biographical information. He sent the following:

BORN: May 15th, 1894, in North London. Father was Welsh, son of a shepherd, self-taught, came to London and became a very minor civil servant—a scrivener of legal documents. A deeply religious man. Mother born in King's Cross, London, was one of thirteen children, their father a shoemaker and small shopkeeper. I was the youngest of three boys, the middle one also still living, and we had a younger sister.

EDUCATED: State school and grammar before leaving for Australia. After the war, was given a choice of re-education by a grateful government and went for journalism. Passed the high-pressure arts course at London University.

MARRIED: Twice. First during the First World War, and widowed in the Second. One daughter, now married and emigrated to Australia, and one son, shot down at nineteen years of age in a bombing raid over Germany. Second marriage during the Second World War. One son and two daughters, all married and living in England, two with baby boys.

HOBBIES: Sport of every kind to watch and write about. Golf to play. Travel, both to enjoy and write about. Newspapers!

BRIEF HISTORY: Arriving home in December 1914, I joined a heavy artillery Territorial unit, and after training on 9.2 guns I was drafted to a Thames-side anti-aircraft battery, manning a pompom firing two-inch shells with a range of two thousand feet at Zeppelins flying at six thousand feet. My father used his Welsh influence to get me a commission in the Royal Welch Fusiliers, but this was delayed for several months because I had led a

213

mutiny, the second in my life, against sheer boredom on the Essex marshes.

Action in France on the Somme. Promoted to captain only because the battalion lined up ninety-strong out of eight hundred after the 1917 Ypres battle. Mentioned in dispatches for no reason except that there were so few left to receive the ration.

After the war, two years' university training and trying to earn a living writing fiction. In 1921 went into Fleet Street, freelancing, and soon found a staff job on a new daily. This was "merged" after a few years and I joined the London *Evening News*, where I really learned the hard way about writing for a living. But the bush had inculcated a love of working (or living without work) for myself, and I left a good staff job at thirty-nine years of age to start a Fleet Street sports news agency.

Have been free ever since, and still have a publishing business with an address off Fleet Street and still retain membership of the London Press Club. Became Captain Cuttle of the BBC from 1937 to 1943. My office was bombed three times, and I then joined Lord Reith in the Ministry of Works as public relations officer (stone the crows!).

After *this* war my second wife, Brenda, and I decided to publish a magazine for parents. Gradually this flourished and we became quite a sound publishing company. I wrote an article called "For fathers only" every month, a light article about the family, and in these, as well as in my bedside chats to the children, I often told stories of the bush. Indeed, my last salute at nights was always ". . . and no bush jokes". This is still a family password.

We are now retired, as much as we ever shall be, having sold off *Parents* but retained our travel annual to keep us in touch. Our son is now a director and is gradually taking the load off our shoulders. Our eldest daughter at twenty-two went alone to Australia to check up on some of my tales, and worked as a jilleroo on an up-country sheep station in South Australia. The other daughter, having spread her wings alone, just as our son did at twenty years old, in the United States, is now with BBC Television, has scripted parts of *Crow On A Barbed Wire Fence* and is eager for a chance to script the whole book.

I now have, in and around Adelaide, one sister-in-law, one daughter plus husband, three grandchildren, two great-grandchildren, one niece plus husband and their two sons. This is why I like to visit Adelaide every other year or so.

When we sold *Parents* my wife said: "You've been telling us so much about the bush all these years, why the hell don't you write a book about it, now that you have some time to spare?" So I did. The bush and its bushwhackers are dearest to my heart after my family. You can't work in the Outback without gaining enormous respect for those who live there and learn to like it.

Why don't I go back? Well, I tried a few years ago. In London I booked planes to Singapore, Darwin, Mt Isa, some other place I've forgotten (Cloncurry?) and Longreach, where I intended taking whatever one could take to Muttaburra. What happened? I arrived at Darwin twenty-two hours late, thus missing the whole chain of connecting flights.

So I gave it up. "Just as well," an old-timer told me. "First it would have killed you" (it was mid-January) ". . . and second, if Muttaburra is true to form, there's nothing there beyond a row of petrol pumps." Still, I reckon it would have been worth the effort, if only to see the crows sitting on those pumps.

HAROLD LEWIS
January, 1973